The Active
Teacher

This book is dedicated to my grandmother, Miriam Love Nash, for whose unconditional love and consistent support I shall be forever grateful.

The Active Teacher

Practical Strategies for Maximizing Teacher Effectiveness

Ron Nash

CORWIN
A SAGE Company

For information:

Corwin
A SAGE Company
2455 Teller Road
Thousand Oaks, California 91320
(800) 233-9936
Fax: (800) 417-2466
www.corwinpress.com

SAGE Ltd.
1 Oliver's Yard
55 City Road
London EC1Y 1SP
United Kingdom

SAGE Pvt. Ltd.
B 1/I 1 Mohan Cooperative
  Industrial Area
Mathura Road, New Delhi 110 044
India

SAGE Asia-Pacific Pte. Ltd.
33 Pekin Street #02-01
Far East Square
Singapore 048763

Printed in the United States of America

Library of Congress Cataloging-in-Publication Data

Nash, Ron, 1949-
The active teacher: practical strategies for maximizing teacher effectiveness/Ron Nash; foreword by Fredric H. Jones.
     p. cm.
Includes bibliographical references and index.
ISBN 978-1-4129-7387-8 (pbk.)
    1. Classroom management. 2. Teacher-student relationships. 3. Active learning. I. Title.

LB3013.N27 2009
371.102′4—dc22   2009002807

This book is printed on acid-free paper.

09   10   11   12   13   10   9   8   7   6   5   4   3   2   1

Acquisitions Editor:	Hudson Perigo
Editorial Assistant:	Lesley K. Blake
Production Editor:	Veronica Stapleton
Copy Editor:	Jenifer Dill
Typesetter:	C&M Digitals (P) Ltd.
Proofreader:	Dennis W. Webb
Indexer:	Sheila Bodell
Cover Designer:	Karine Hovsepian

Contents

Foreword

In *The Active Teacher*, Ron Nash brings his extensive experience in teaching, supervision, and staff development to the task of improving classroom instruction. What makes his approach so powerful is the broad and holistic way he envisions change. After identifying barriers to success in the classroom, he conceptualizes remedies both within the classroom and at the school-site level.

Mr. Nash focuses on areas of classroom teaching that reduce teacher stress while shifting the workload to the students. Upset is replaced with calmness, mobility, and effective body language. Nagging is replaced with teaching routines to mastery. Lecturing is replaced with interactive learning as checking for understanding becomes a continuous process of collaboration with the student. The role of the teacher that emerges is one of facilitator, coach, and consultant.

At the school-site level, Mr. Nash examines the challenges of replacing teacher isolation with collaboration. The desire for professional growth is not easily transformed into a process of renewal. Commitment must be wed to a stepwise plan that embodies effective procedure. Forces that tend toward the status quo can overwhelm the desire for innovation without a process that leads the faculty forward. Of equal importance, what motivates teachers to seek professional growth, and what de-motivates them?

This book is a valuable resource in both preservice and inservice programs. It not only supplies a wealth of effective teaching practices, but it also provides a guide to successful functioning as a member of a learning community.

Fredric H. Jones, PhD

Prologue

Meet Trey.

Having graduated from a nearby college in May, Trey began his teaching career in August at a middle school in a city of about 120,000 people. His assignment was eighth-grade world history, and he was one of four core teachers on an eighth-grade team. Trey had no contact with the school during the summer and first saw his classroom when all the teachers reported for work the week prior to the opening of school. On Monday of that inservice week, Trey met his official mentor, who greeted him with an invitation to "call me if you have questions!" Trey neither saw nor heard from his mentor for the rest of the week.

Trey was early for his first eighth-grade team meeting on Tuesday morning, but two of the three other team members were late and complained loudly about their schedules and the condition of their classrooms after the summer break. The meeting was short, and Trey did not mind; he used the rest of the morning to put up his first bulletin board and look over his faculty manual, a lengthy document that seemed to mostly include school policies and procedures. After tracking down another social studies teacher, he finally located his world history curriculum guide.

Friday afternoon, the principal brought the staff together in the library to introduce various members of the nonteaching staff and to walk the faculty through the manual section by section. The principal made a pointed reference to the need to get into course content quickly in September because of low state test scores the previous year. He went on talking for some time in a meeting that lasted three hours, including a ten-minute break that stretched to twenty minutes. Trey noticed more than one teacher, including a member of his own team, looking over class lists or doing their own work, seemingly oblivious to the principal's message. After the break, a few teachers simply did not return to the meeting. The meeting adjourned with the principal's request that they get plenty of rest over the weekend and arrive on time on Monday, the first day of school for students.

Trey, determined to follow his principal's instructions and hit the ground running with content, handed out textbooks on the first day and then plunged into the world history curriculum. September went fairly smoothly, but by October there were signs that all was not well on his team. Team meetings were devoted to discipline problems, and playing the blame game was the order of the day. Trey, who always considered himself a positive person, came to dread the meetings and the negativity that predominated.

Worse, by late November, Trey's own classroom discipline had broken down; each day was a struggle. The amount of homework turned in by students had steadily declined over the past several weeks, and the number of negative phone calls home had increased to two per week. One parent he called did not even seem to know who Trey was. The winter break was a welcome relief, but Trey did not look forward to January and what promised to be a long second semester.

With some time to reflect in late December, Trey concluded that he was on a dysfunctional team in a dysfunctional school. February and March brought frequent thoughts of quitting teaching altogether. He was offered a sales position in a thriving retail business by a family friend, and his parents encouraged him to do what was best for him and for his future. As April arrived, Trey had some decisions to make and three big questions to answer: (1) How had this gone so wrong? (2) What could he have done differently to affect the outcome? and (3) Would he sign a teaching contract in May for the next school year?

Trey decided he was going to have to work on his own to change things for the better, and he began talking with veteran teachers in his school who were well respected and whose students consistently performed well. He also began to read books on classroom management and found several online articles on classroom climate, formative assessment, collaboration, and the characteristics of effective teachers. In his reading, he discovered evidence that teachers have more of an impact on student success than any other single factor. He had listened to his teammates play the blame game all year long and realized that if he returned next year he would have to find a way to insulate himself from the negativity that seemed to predominate in so many corners of the building.

In May, just before teaching contracts were issued by the principal, Trey decided to return for a second year in the classroom. He also made a decision to spend the summer adjusting his whole approach to teaching and learning in his classroom, instituting new processes and instructional delivery methods that would benefit a new group of students and, perhaps, jumpstart his own career.

Preface

Mrs. Randall's day went from bad to worse five minutes into the first class of the day. She had spent much of the night awake and had subsequently slept through her alarm. Having arrived to school late, she was not totally prepared for the thirty seventh graders in her first period class. The kids were more wound up than usual, and at the five-minute mark, Eddie stepped hard on her last nerve. Throwing the whiteboard eraser down on the floor, Mrs. Randall screamed, "Shut up! All of you just shut up!" The students did stop talking, but she quickly realized she had made a major mistake. The shock on their faces soon turned to sullen resentment, and their body language showed everything from amazement to embarrassment, and even disgust. Mrs. Randall realized that in the space of a few seconds, she had perhaps significantly damaged relationships she had spent the last months working to build. It was an expensive misstep, one that could carry a heavy price.

Mrs. Randall calmed down, took a couple of deep breaths, apologized to the entire class for her outburst, and reminded them that such loss of control is not professional and not the kind of behavior she expected from herself or from her students. After class, she had a short conversation with Eddie about his behavior. She even took the step of explaining to her subsequent classes how she had lost her temper and discussing with them how damaging such loss of control can be on the classroom environment.

Our fictional Mrs. Randall is a good teacher—one who prides herself on her ability to remain calm in the face of adversity. Having made what she recognized could be a costly error, she worked to repair the damage and get things back to normal. She even involved her classes in a reflective conversation about just how expensive such outbursts can be. They discussed how such behavior on the part of a teacher can get students quiet in the short run—but at an unacceptably high cost that most certainly could involve a diminution of trust. She and her students learned something from the experience and moved on.

In *Tools for Teaching*, Fred Jones (2007) encourages teachers to always "keep it cheap." In saying this, Jones is not talking about money, but about the fact that there are moments when we can save time and effort yet achieve the same end. Why, for example, go all the way across a classroom to get a student to quit disrupting others when a meaningful look from a distance will get the job done (p. 198)? Simply "looking the student back to work" involves less time and effort than walking across the room—yet it gets the same results. The walk is unnecessary if the look will suffice. Few things are more precious to teachers than time, and time is one of many things related to teaching that can either be squandered or wisely spent.

Teachers who lecture for the greater part of a class period may find that it helps cover the curriculum in the short haul, but in the end this coverage comes at the expense of student engagement and understanding. According to Feinstein (2004), while lecture "can be an efficient way to deliver instruction," it lacks an emotional connection to students (p. 19). Most kids (and adults for that matter) neither enjoy nor learn better while sitting still and listening to a teacher or college instructor talk for long periods of time. Most educators have observed what Hannaford (2005) calls "the glazed eyes and vacant stares of students in a lecture hall or classroom" (p. 54). Yet lecture continues to be a popular instructional delivery method, especially at the secondary and college level.

My experience has been that students in the middle and upper grades have developed a marvelous ability to "play the game." By that I mean that they will look at the teacher and smile several minutes into a lecture, when in fact they punched out long ago and may well be engaged in mental activities totally unrelated to the curriculum. In my first two years of teaching, I totally misread those smiles. Because I wanted to think it was true, I believed the smiles meant the students were with me. I often tested that thinking by asking, periodically, whether they had any questions. Usually, there were no questions, and I assumed that my students were processing as I lectured and that they understood every word and concept. It never occurred to me that, mentally, they had gone to another place entirely and that, for the most part, I was having a great discussion with myself. Clearly, I was not engaging my students. My lectures, while well-meaning, were far too expensive *because they gave me (and them) little in the way of a return on my investment.*

These three situations—losing one's temper in front of students, crossing a crowded room to intervene with a student, and lecturing almost exclusively as a way of covering the content—are examples of investing too much to get too little in return. At best, little is accomplished in each case. At worst, the effects of such actions can be academically harmful and, as in the case of our Mrs. Randall, can damage personal relationships and create an unsafe classroom environment. Let's look at each of the three situations with an eye toward investing much less (keeping it cheap) and getting a much greater return on our investment. If time is of the essence and if, therefore, every minute in class should be used wisely, how could each of these negatives be turned into a positive?

In the case of Mrs. Randall, had she just taken a couple of deep breaths before doing or saying anything, she could no doubt have handled the situation much differently. Had she, for example, simply raised her right hand (her regular signal for getting the attention of her seventh graders), in all likelihood the students would have responded positively *and she would not have had to say anything at all.* Simply raising her hand would have helped her keep it cheap. At the very least, a teacher who loses her temper creates a climate of fear in the classroom. Also, students who perceive this loss of control as outright aggression may react in an aggressive manner, making a bad situation much worse (Bailey, 2000, p. 106).

As for lecture, if it is used effectively—that is, if short periods of teacher talk are followed by time for student processing—then understanding will be served and students will be far more likely to remember what they processed. Jensen (2005) affirms that providing "time to discuss in pairs or small groups the relevance of new information" assists in the construction of meaning for students (p. 12). If lengthy lectures and a lack of in-class processing of new information result in little understanding and retention, it is too expensive. In classrooms dominated by lecture and teacher talk, teachers do too much of the work while students do too little.

After nearly four decades in education, I have come to the conclusion that—in the most successful classrooms—the *kids* do most of the work and the teachers facilitate process. The teachers in these classrooms provide frequent and meaningful feedback, shift the work load to the students, and ask more questions than they attempt to answer; *by doing all these things, they keep it cheap.* In the least successful classrooms, the teachers do most of the work and get little return on their investment. These less-successful teachers spend large amounts of classroom time lecturing, explaining, reminding, cajoling, and reacting (often badly) to disruptive students. My experience has been that, sooner or later, these teachers become victims of their own expensive and often debilitating mistakes. As the mistakes and the resulting expenditures pile up, teachers begin to rethink their commitment to teaching, and students begin to rethink their commitment to learning.

How many teachers simply decide the price is too steep? How many teachers go it alone, without a mentor and with little support, until it just becomes too much to bear? How many, at a relatively young age, turn in the keys to their classroom and simply walk away from teaching? This is not, as the saying goes, rocket science. A teacher who is fundamentally unhappy and does not look forward to coming to school every day will find the cost of doing business in the schoolhouse too expensive. By the same token, a student who is fundamentally unhappy and does not look forward to coming to school every day will find the cost of doing business in the classroom too expensive—he or she will just shut down and, perhaps along with the teacher, become yet another casualty.

Wise investments can be frontloaded in terms of establishing smooth-running processes and creating "an emotionally safe school climate" (Bluestein, 2001, p. 12). Teachers who spend the first week of school on basic classroom procedures (e.g., transitions, working effectively in pairs and teams, and using time efficiently) will be able to keep it cheap the rest of the year. Wong and Wong (2005) affirm that students, especially those who come from dysfunctional home environments, need "something familiar and secure that they can rely on" (p. 191). Just as early monetary investments ensure a comfortable retirement income, early investments in the area of efficient processes and relationship building will pay off all year long for teachers and students alike. Investing up front allows teachers to keep it cheap in the classroom when every minute—and every action—counts. Investing up front in the basics and then sidestepping costly mistakes along the way will help teachers facilitate process and progress in the classroom. This thoughtful investment of time and effort may also serve to keep teachers from becoming victims of burnout, something that leads many to simply pack it all in and leave the teaching profession.

I make no claim that classrooms can be transformed into perfect places, yet it is my belief that teachers can and should enjoy teaching and that students can and should enjoy learning. When this is the case, classrooms can be wonderful and exciting places.

In the Prologue, we met Trey, a new teacher who experienced a great deal of frustration during his first year in his middle school. Many of his problems resulted from a lack of meaningful support from his administration and his middle-school-team colleagues. Trey's teacher mentor told Trey to call him if he had questions. The problem, of course, is that *brand new teachers may not know what questions are worth asking.* Near the end of his first year teaching, Trey began to seek out successful teachers in his school, with whom he had substantive discussions, and he began to spend time reading professional journals and books—which convinced him that a second year did not have to be as frustrating as the first. Trey discovered through his research and conversations that he had made fundamental errors that served as impediments to improvement for both himself and his students. He made a commitment to frontload his second year in such a way that he could avoid the mistakes that had proved costly the first time around.

This book explores eight components of successful classrooms. It is quite likely Trey would have been more successful had he been aware of the importance of having clear and consistent procedures and rules in place from the first day of school. Chapter 1 deals with these process-related issues. Chapter 2 follows up with another critical foundational issue: building relationships with students, parents, and members of the adult school community. An important part of building sustainable relationships is the ability to stay calm and avoid losing one's temper, and Chapter 3 is devoted to the issue of building trust by cultivating a safe classroom environment. These first three chapters are critical to creating the kind of classroom climate where teachers and students can operate and collaborate on a daily basis, free of the kind of inconsistencies and lack of trust that exist in too many classrooms.

Students want to be part of the action, and the idea of sitting day after day and month after month watching their teachers work is, not to put too fine a point on it, *not motivating, satisfying, or productive.* Chapter 4 serves to bridge the gap between process and content by demonstrating the importance of shifting the workload from teacher to student by engaging students meaningfully in the learning process. Chapter 5 tackles the important role of feedback in improving the academic performance of students. Chapter 6 extends this exploration of the nature and uses of feedback by looking at the balance between summative and formative assessment.

One of Trey's problems was the fact that his middle-school-team partners were not really interested in meeting on a regular basis, and they were even less interested in solving problems and ramping up instructional effectiveness for the team's students. Chapter 7 focuses on the importance of collaboration in the continuous improvement process.

Relevance is often in the eye of the beholder, and the beholders show up every August or September expecting that what we as teachers want them to do in school will connect with what they are going to need after graduation. The final chapter, Chapter 8, is devoted to the critical issue of the relevance of *what* we teach in school, *how* we teach it, and *why* we teach it.

The second year of Trey's career was resuscitated, as we have seen, by his willingness to take charge and approach the coming school year with a proactive, rather than reactive, approach. Later in the book we will discover that Trey's teaching career takes a further upturn as . . . well . . . first things first.

Acknowledgments

Over the years, I have had the privilege of observing teachers in well over three hundred classrooms at all grade levels. These classroom visits and the subsequent conversations with those teachers have deepened my understanding of the art and science of teaching. From other professionals in the field of education, I have gleaned much else about the learning process. I thank those teachers for welcoming me into their classrooms, and I appreciate the assistance and advice of many other educators who have contributed to what is for me a continual work in progress.

I thank my editor at Corwin, Hudson Perigo, as well as her editorial assistant Lesley Blake, for their constant encouragement and assistance throughout the writing process. Special thanks go to my copy editor, Jenifer Dill, for her thorough and thoughtful assistance in the process of proofing the book. Indeed, all the fine professionals at Corwin have my sincere thanks for their continual efforts on my behalf.

Most important, I thank my wife Candy for her constant support of my second career as a consultant and author. I am forever grateful to her.

Additionally, Corwin wishes to acknowledge the following peer reviewers for their editorial insight and guidance.

Dr. Nora Alder
Associate Professor
Virginia Commonwealth
 University
Richmond, VA

Nicolette Dennis
Principal
Highland High School
Albuquerque, NM

Tanya Marcinkewicz
Sixth-Grade Teacher
Harlan Elementary School
Wilmington, DE

Kathryn McCormick
Seventh-Grade Teacher,
    NBCT
Gahanna Middle School East
Gahanna, OH

Rachel McMillan
Literacy Coach
Corporate Landing Middle
    School
Virginia Beach Public
    Schools
Virginia Beach, VA

Paulette E. Mills, PhD
Associate Professor,
    Department of Teaching
    and Learning
Washington State University
Pullman, WA

Phyllis Milne, EdD
Associate Director of
    Curriculum and Student
    Achievement
York County School
    Division
Yorktown, VA

Lauren Mittermann, NBCT
Social Studies Teacher
Gibraltar Area Schools
Fish Creek, WI

Lori Musser
Elementary School Principal
Columbia Elementary School
Joplin, MO

Ricka Peterson
Learning Specialist
St. Paul's School
Brooklandville, MD

Brett Piersma
Teacher
Santa Ynez Valley Union
    High School
Santa Ynez, CA

Jonathan Plucker
Professor of Educational
    Psychology
Indiana University
Bloomington, IN

Fredricka K. Reisman, PhD
Interim Associate Dean for
    Research
Godwin College of
    Professional Studies,
    Drexel University
Philadelphia, PA

Rosemary Traoré
Assistant Professor, Urban
    Education
University of North
    Carolina at Charlotte
Charlotte, NC

Shelley Joan Weiss
Principal
Waunakee Community
    Middle School
Waunakee, WI

About the Author

**Ron Nash** is the author of the Corwin bestseller *The Active Classroom* (2008), a book dedicated to shifting students from passive observers to active participants in their own learning. Ron's professional career in education has included teaching social studies at the middle and high school levels. He also served as an instructional coordinator and organizational development specialist for the Virginia Beach City Public Schools for thirteen years. In that capacity, Ron trained thousands of teachers and other school division employees in such varied topics as classroom management, instructional strategies, presentation techniques, relationship building, customer service, and process management. After Ron's retirement from the Virginia Beach City Public Schools in 2007, he founded Ron Nash and Associates, Inc., a company dedicated to working with teachers in the area of brain-compatible learning. Originally from Pennsylvania, Ron and his wife Candy, a French teacher, have lived in Virginia Beach for the past twenty-four years. Ron can be reached through his Web site at www.ronnashandassociates.com.

Introduction

This book takes care of some unfinished business from the final chapter of my first book, *The Active Classroom* (2008), in which I briefly surfaced several obstacles to effective instruction. These included unclear or inconsistent rules and procedures, an overreliance on lecture and summative assessments, negativity in the classroom, along with a tendency toward insular teaching, and an avoidance of collegiality and purposeful collaboration both in the classroom and in the schoolhouse. The intent of *The Active Teacher* is to explore these and other critical themes as they relate to student achievement, classroom climate, instruction, assessment, and student motivation.

The central idea of this book is that teachers who enter the school year and simply react to events put themselves in a much more precarious position than teachers who spend a good deal of time thinking ahead and planning for what *might* happen in the classroom, as well as reflecting on what *could* be for students. Teachers who make the choice to wait on events each day while working in virtual isolation may find the going tough and the consequences prohibitively expensive. It is not necessary for teachers to spend their day in reactive mode, and there is no need for teachers to isolate themselves from those who can and will help if asked. We'll discover in this book that there are plenty of opportunities for collaboration for those who seek a collegial, rather than insular, approach to the teaching profession.

Finally, teachers who attend to the three Rs (i.e., routines, rules, and relationships) during the first week of school are more likely to be successful than those who jump into course content before laying a procedural foundation. Not spending sufficient time on preparation and process can lead to confusion, misapprehension, and uncertainty on the part of students. These unintended and unhappy consequences *are not cost effective;* they will ultimately serve as de-motivators for students and teachers alike.

Truly active teachers are not content to wait on events. Rather, they are teachers who plan, prepare, and predict what might happen so that they will be ready for whatever comes their way. Having planned the work, these teachers now work the plan—managing and evaluating process at every turn and making midcourse adjustments on a continuous improvement journey that never ends.

Those readers who have read my first book, *The Active Classroom,* or who have been with me as participants in my workshops, will recognize "Eddie," the fictitious student who, perhaps, assisted in turning my hair prematurely gray. In fact, there is a whole cast of fictitious characters in this book, whom I shall call upon from time to time to help demonstrate a point or tell a story. I subscribe to the theory that storytelling is a powerful and informative teacher; there are many stories to be told and, I trust, many lessons to be learned in the pages that follow.

1

Positioning
First Things First

I once observed an elementary teacher leading her kids down a long hallway on their way to the cafeteria. Along the way, two of the students started talking, and the teacher turned to face the group as she walked backwards in front of them. She raised her hand with her palm facing them, and the line of students came to an abrupt halt. With both hands, she pointed back down the hallway whence they had come. The students turned and quietly walked back to her classroom. When they reached the doorway, they once again turned around and started down the hallway to the cafeteria—this time without a sound.

The teacher's body language was totally neutral. Raising her hand, stopping the students with a practiced gesture, and then pointing back down the hallway were all process—as opposed to punishment—tools. She did not yell, scold, or nag. Her face displayed absolutely no displeasure at all. She did not send someone to time-out or embarrass anyone. In fact, she never said a word during the entire scenario, but her message was clear—*we move quietly through the hallway and when we don't get it right, we practice until we do*—and they understood. In this case, perfect practice made for a perfect procedure, and it worked because this teacher had perfected the *how* of moving thirty kids down the hallway without disturbing other classes in the process.

In teaching, there is the *what* and the *how*. The *what* is the course content, and it is necessary that teachers demonstrate command of their discipline(s). The *how* is more about process (i.e., the procedures and methods that facilitate the smooth functioning of the classroom). A teacher who knows his content but fails to consider the critical role of process is much more likely to experience problems. A truly successful teacher is one who constantly reflects on the *how* because she understands the value of certainty, clarity, and consistency in an effective classroom.

In almost four decades in education, and after observing hundreds of classrooms, there is one thing I believe with utter certainty—students hate uncertainty as it relates to process. They want to know exactly where they stand at all times. Students want to know what to do when they have questions and when they need to sharpen a pencil. They need to know what to do when they enter a teacher's classroom and what is expected when it is time to clean up from a lab. Students want to know that if the teacher promises to have test results back within three days, it will happen. They want to believe that they will be shown the same respect by their teachers that their teachers demand of them. They want to know they will get meaningful feedback as a matter of course, aimed at letting them know where they stand and highlighting what they need to do in order to get to where they are going. Good teachers approach each year with an understanding of how important procedures are in day-to-day classroom operations. Ambiguity and inconsistency inhibit the smooth flow of process in the classroom.

Students need to know with utter certainty that if they participate in class discussions, they can do so without fear of ridicule from fellow students. If they cannot do so, they will not contribute. Teachers must constantly consider how they will handle students who test the limits and break the rules. Students want to know that the rules on the wall are not there for show. I have been in classrooms where there is a long list of rules posted prominently somewhere in the room, every one of which was broken by the students (and ignored by the teachers) in the space of a very few minutes. I have seen classrooms where the teacher broke his or her own rules, thereby destroying their efficacy.

According to Emmer, Evertson, and Worsham (2003), "inefficient procedures and the absence of routines . . . can waste large amounts of time and cause students' attention and interest to wane" (p. 17). Procedures that are both understood and followed on a daily basis contribute to the smooth running of the classroom.

The Role of Rules

Wong and Wong (2005), in *How to Be an Effective Teacher: The First Days of School*, spend three out of a total of twenty-six chapters illuminating the critical differences between rules and procedures, and the authors recommend that teachers read all three chapters in one sitting so that the distinction will be clear. Rules, according to Wong and Wong "are expectations of appropriate student behavior" (p. 143), and they distinguish between general rules (e.g., respect others) and specific rules (e.g., arrive to class on time) (p. 145).

Smith (2004) goes one step further to distinguish principles, which "are more general and often more value-laden than rules"; an example he provides is that "students have the right to learn and the teacher has the right to teach" (p. 164). Further, Smith describes rules as "what we would see in the classroom if our principles were being supported" (p. 165). To Smith, a rule that says one should not interrupt others supports the student's right to learn and the teacher's right to teach (p. 65). Thorson (2003), on the basis of interviews conducted with students serving detention, says rules should be few in number and should be positively and clearly worded.

One way to make certain that there are no misunderstandings about principles, rules, consequences, or procedures is to engage students in substantive discussions about their ultimate importance and their necessity in the smooth running of the classroom. Curwin (2003) suggests that involving students directly in the creation of rules for themselves and for the teacher "begins the process of developing a classroom community" (p. 81). Di Giulio (2007) emphasizes that in a successful classroom community teachers are proactive in that they "involve their students in creating the rules by providing an opportunity for them to think about, discuss, and put into action positive expectations for human behavior" (p. 20). Involving students in these critical discussions helps develop and nurture the kind of classroom climate that will pay dividends down the road.

The fact that students have input into the rule-creating process gives them a sense of ownership that might otherwise be lacking. This is supported in the results of a study by Brophy and Evertson (1976) in which they concluded that "more successful teachers took pains to explain both the rule itself and the reason behind it to the children" (as quoted in Marzano, 2003a, p. 16). Marzano (2003a) affirms that research and theory, then, support the intuitive notion that well-articulated rules and procedures that are negotiated with students are a critical aspect of classroom management, affecting not only the behavior of students but also their academic achievement. (p. 17)

One very practical reason for taking time during the first week of school to explain and discuss rules is that students have several other teachers who may have slightly different rules; therefore, simply announcing what the rules are may not be sufficient. Consequences also need to be clear and well-understood. New teachers or teachers new to a building need to discover how school-wide rules and consequences will affect those developed in the classroom. Any discussion on rules and consequences must include school norms and dictates that will affect those developed in the classroom. The same may apply to procedures. Simply announcing what the procedures are is therefore not sufficient. The teacher's job is to have students practice these procedures *until they become second nature in that particular class-room.* This can take time, and teachers must be absolutely consistent in their actions regarding procedures. Teachers must be relentless in seeing to it that the procedures are both understood and followed consistently.

When teachers treat procedures as process related and not consequence laden, it can also have a positive effect on relationships by cutting down on flashpoints (e.g., the child who gets up to sharpen his pencil without asking when the procedure is to get permission) that can lead to *direct* and *negative* confrontations between teachers and students. A procedure not followed becomes simply an opportunity to reteach it to an individual student or to the class as a whole, not as an occasion for a public verbal reprimand that can result in derailing an entire lesson.

Facilitating Process

Students and teachers alike want to see classrooms run smoothly. Students appreciate not only being involved in the development of classroom rules, then, but they also want to be involved directly in their own learning throughout the school year. Students understandably prefer being actively engaged to watching teachers lecture. For a teacher, then, the question becomes, *How do I move kids from passive observers to active participants without it resulting in chaos?* Part of the answer lies in understanding how effective procedures (process) can satisfy a student's need for certainty, clarity, and consistency. Effective procedures, as we have seen, do not simply happen. The investment is frontloaded as students are introduced to a procedure and then practice it until it becomes routine.

An example might help explain this.

> *Mrs. Dalrymple stands in the doorway to her seventh-grade English class greeting students, who enter the room to the song "Get Ready," by the Temptations, which is playing on Mrs. Dalrymple's CD player. Students glance at the TV monitor in the corner of the room and see a picture of a student's desk with three items displayed: a blank sheet of paper, a sharpened pencil, and a book of short stories. Each student tears a blank sheet of paper out of his or her notebook, places a sharpened pencil on the desk, and goes to the book shelf in the back of the room to get a copy of the book of short stories. With one last glance at the TV monitor to make sure they have everything, the students take their seats. Mrs. Dalrymple moves from the doorway into the room. She uses the remote in her hand to bring the volume of the music up a bit and then she stops the music abruptly. The students, who have been chatting while they collected what they will need for the lesson, stop talking and give Mrs. Dalrymple their full attention, ready to begin.*
>
> *Near the end of the lesson, Mrs. Dalrymple picks up her remote and plays "I Can See Clearly Now," by Johnny Nash. She says nothing and gives no instructions, but the students see that the TV monitor now shows the bookshelf with the books in order by number. (Each book has a small, numbered sticker on the bottom of the spine.) Without being asked, the students return the books and get their desks cleaned off while listening to the music. After a minute or so, Mrs. Dalrymple raises the volume and then cuts it off, and the students once more give her their attention.*

In the above example, notice that Mrs. Dalrymple never actually *said* anything, yet the students were ready to start the lesson on cue. At the end of the lesson, Mrs. Dalrymple gave no verbal instructions, yet the students were in their seats and ready to leave the classroom. Also, notice that it was a combination of an auditory cue (a specific song) and a visual cue (a picture on the TV monitor) that got the results Mrs. Dalrymple wanted. Her investment in this whole process came well in advance of the first week of school. Let's go back with her to early August, when she frontloads the procedures that will help facilitate the smooth operation of her classroom when her students arrive.

1. As she begins her preparations, Mrs. Dalrymple chooses two songs that she will use when she wants students to set up their desks for instruction or clean up after an activity or near the end of class: "Get Ready" and "I Can See Clearly Now."

2. After borrowing the school's digital camera, she takes a series of digital photos of the top of a student desk. Each picture captures a different setup (an empty desk, a desk with a pencil and a blank sheet of paper, a desk with a textbook, etc.).

3. She then hooks her classroom computer up to her TV monitor so she can display anything from the computer on the screen. She also numbers the short-story books on her bookshelf so they can be put back in the proper order by the students.

4. On the first day of class, Mrs. Dalrymple explains to the students that she will be using music as an auditory cue for certain routines. She then plays about thirty seconds of "Get Ready" and indicates that the only time they will hear that particular song is when there is something on the TV monitor that indicates how their desks should look.

5. She then plays about thirty seconds of "I Can See Clearly Now" and explains that this song will be played at the end of the class or when a general cleanup is warranted. Once again, this will be accompanied by an image on the TV monitor that will provide visual direction.

6. Mrs. Dalrymple then has the students practice setting up their desks using the songs and the images on the TV monitor. She stresses that book bags, jackets, and purses sitting on desks simply get in the way, so practicing desk setup also includes stowing everything personal under the desks and out of the way. On their second effort, she times them and then they work to improve that time.

7. On the second day of school, Mrs. Dalrymple stands in the doorway as students enter the room. With "Get Ready" playing, she observes how many of them remember the auditory and visual cues. Once again, they practice this procedure until by the end of the first week of school it has become routine.

Any teacher who has given a set of auditory directions to students knows very well that those directions may have to be repeated because someone (perhaps more than one someone) did not hear them. Mrs. Dalrymple, having done just that for years, decided to add the visual component and the musical cue, *basically taking her out of the equation.* She discovered she could now greet students as they entered, safe in the knowledge that inside the room, desks were being set up as required. The picture on the TV monitor leaves no room for uncertainty. Every desk simply needs to look like that!

She has also discovered that this saves time. Shortly after she enters the room, her students are ready to go. The *responsibility* for desk setup rests with them, not with Mrs. Dalrymple. All this is done without any intervention on her part other than raising the volume of the music before cutting it off, something that gets their attention. Once again, investing early in process pays big dividends later on.

Here is one more example of frontloading process in order to make things run smoothly down the road.

The students in Mr. McGrath's high school social studies class have just listened to a ten-minute story about one of Harriet Tubman's trips as a conductor on the Underground Railroad. Mr. McGrath then asks each student to look around the room and locate his or her 3:00 partner. That done, Mr. McGrath plays an upbeat song while the students stand and pair up. He raises the volume a bit and then cuts it off, effectively getting their attention. He then says, "Talk with your partner about the story. Bring up with your partner any questions you might like to ask of me." As they begin to talk, Mr. McGrath plays another piece of music on his CD player.

While students talk, Mr. McGrath walks around and listens to the conversations and to the questions being posed. He makes a mental note of two good questions and asks those two students if they would be willing to share their questions with the entire class. Then he raises the volume of the music, cuts it off, and the students thank each other before returning to their seats. Once they are seated, he asks the two students who agreed to share to go ahead and do that. Mr. McGrath charts the questions without answering them and then asks for more. With an eventual list of six questions, he begins a general discussion of the material.

Once again, what did the teacher, Mr. McGrath, do to permit such a smooth transition from the story to the student pairing to the sharing?

1. During the first week of school, Mr. McGrath has students choose clock partners, so that each student has a permanent 12:00, 3:00, 6:00, and 9:00 partner. During that first week, he has them stand and meet with each of those partners in turn and asks them to discuss something having to do with themselves (e.g., favorite vacations, food, movies, or music). His purpose during those first few days is to get them used to talking to each other.

2. He also introduces them to the idea that music will accompany them to their partners and get them back to their seats. Music will also, he explains, be playing while they talk in order to make their conversations more private.

3. In the course of getting them used to this pair/share procedure, he has them acknowledge their partners repeatedly by thanking them before returning to their seats. He thus gets them into the habit of thanking each other *without being prompted.*

4. Finally, he explains to his students during that first week that he will try to keep any lectures or periods of "teacher talk" to no more than about ten minutes, after which they will have the opportunity to process the information with a partner or in a trio.

In the two examples above, Mrs. Dalrymple and Mr. McGrath committed to spending several days allowing students to become totally familiar with process. They understood that it is not enough to tell students how things will be—students must experience it and practice it until it becomes routine. In classroom after classroom where I observe that students are comfortable with routine and things run smoothly, teachers admit to spending a good deal of time in the first few days of school putting the process horse before the content cart.

Let's go to elementary school for one more example.

Miss Walsingham uses part of the first day of school to get her fifth graders used to the idea that they will be up and moving much of the time in her classroom. During the course of the day, her twenty-two students stand and pair up on many occasions, always with a different person. The topics of discussion include their favorite weekend activities, their favorite meals, and vacations they would love to take. In the afternoon of that first day, each student is given a card with a topic he or she must explain in detail to a partner. Potential topics might be, What is your favorite time of day and why? or What kind of books do you enjoy reading? or What kind of television programs do you enjoy watching? The listener's job is to summarize what his or her partner said when the answer has been completed.

During that first day, and continuing throughout the opening week of school, Miss Walsingham makes certain that students thank each other for sharing. She indicates that her expectation is that they will offer their own acknowledgment without being prompted. She also indicates that regardless of where they are sitting in the room, students will change partners frequently as they stand and share information during the course of the school year. By the end of the week, Mrs. Walsingham determines that everyone is ready for the introduction of content on the following Monday.

In each of our three examples, and regardless of grade level, the teachers have put process before content; they make certain students get used to talking, sharing, explaining, summarizing, and interacting with every child in the room. By the time subject area content is introduced into the mix, the process basics have been explained, practiced, and internalized. If time is of the essence, then time spent up front streamlining process will pay dividends later in the school year.

Introducing content prior to getting students used to the procedures can have disastrous consequences. I once observed a secondary classroom in which the teacher asked the students to turn to a partner and talk about the previous night's homework (a reading assignment). After a minute or so, the teacher intervened because the conversations were not happening. Several things became apparent to me within that painful minute:

1. The students did not have a regular partner. This first (and essential) part of the process had broken down because students were uncertain about with whom they should pair. The furniture in the room was arranged in such a way that it was difficult for students to move at all. Some students sat more or less alone around the room and could not easily find someone with whom to share.

2. Many of the students had not completed the previous night's reading assignment. Even if they found a partner, therefore, there was little to talk about related to content. This caused some embarrassment on the part of individual students and on the part of the teacher, who had apparently taken it for granted that they had done their homework and was finding out differently.

3. The teacher had obviously not spent time at the beginning of the year preparing the students for the whole idea of conducting student-to-student conversations. Not only were they unprepared in terms of content, they were in unfamiliar territory as it related to process.

Once again, when procedures (processes) become routine, classroom rules (few in number, positively stated, and clearly understood) will stand the test of time. For example, a student who has long ago adopted the *procedure* of standing with his hands at his side while listening quietly (and nonjudgmentally) to a partner in a pair-share activity has begun to master the rule concerning *respectful listening*. Absent efficient procedures, classroom rules are in jeopardy. After observing hundreds of classrooms over the years, I have come to the conclusion that *no matter how many rules are posted on the wall, the lack of effective procedural routine will undermine those rules until behavior spins out of control*. In high-performing classrooms, students know exactly what is expected of them and they do it without complaint or hesitation.

Final Thoughts

Establishing rules and procedures early in the school year, involving students in discussing and understanding the difference between the two, practicing the procedures until they become routine, and being consistent in the application of rules and consequences will help teachers avoid expensive missteps and instead keep it cheap. The course content can wait until the processes are well-established and well-understood.

For the most part, teachers make a fresh start each school year with a new group of students. The kids may be new to that classroom, but they are not new to the educational system. They are veteran students. Their expectations and all they have come to believe about school will accompany them into every new classroom. That sometimes-considerable experience includes teachers who took the time to build relationships and care about them. The students' experience may also include teachers whom the students perceived as more concerned with the content, or any number of other things, than with the students themselves. As teachers plan each summer for that fresh start in August or September, their preparation should include time to determine exactly *how to deposit heavily* in the kinds of relationship accounts that make success far more likely. Chapter 2 deals with this important aspect of building a solid foundation for learning.

2

Investing in Sustainable Relationships

When I was in elementary school, one of my reading teachers, having had a conversation with my grandmother, loaned me a copy of The Tower Treasure, *the very first Hardy Boys mystery. This teacher never missed an opportunity to encourage me in my areas of strength—reading and writing. Her adeptness at communicating with parents and, in my case, grandparents, paid off for both of us. She knew me well and clearly understood my weaknesses and my strengths. It is our strengths that will eventually push or pull us into a given avocation and she understood that. She saw something in me and never missed an opportunity to help me develop in language arts, a subject she knew to be an area of strength for me.*

At the junior/senior high school I attended, I had one English teacher for three separate years—eighth, tenth, and twelfth grades. She knew I liked short stories and never passed up the opportunity to send them my way. She even suggested to my aunt, with whom I lived at the time, that she purchase a two-volume set of Somerset Maugham's short stories as a Christmas present for me, something my aunt promptly did. I still have those two volumes and they are well-marked and much-read. She knew I wanted to be a teacher and counseled me, convincing me to get my masters degree immediately after receiving my BS in Education, if possible. It was possible, and it took me two years with a teaching assistantship; after I graduated with my masters, I went back to my high school and showed her the diploma. I thanked her for the three years in her classroom and for all she had done on my behalf.

This same English teacher used to pass tests back by name in alphabetical order. One day I realized she had somehow missed me in the rotation. I had taken the test, so I knew my paper had to be among those she was distributing. When she walked back to her desk, we were all completing some seatwork and she motioned for me to come up front. Very quietly, she told me that although my grade on tests and quizzes was normally in the A-B range, this particular test score consisted of an uncharacteristically failing grade. She explained that she knew something must be bothering me (it was) and she said she understood that these things happened and I should not be concerned with this grade, which she was sure was an anomaly. I have never forgotten her sensitivity and her discretion. Had she placed that failing paper on my desk in the customary fashion, I would have been visibly upset and she knew it. She showed a great deal of understanding that day and I did—and still do—appreciate her thoughtfulness.

From a distance, then, I can identify several great teachers and professors in my career as a student. I believe every one of them, including the two I have described in the stories above, cared about me as a person. I respected their content knowledge; the fact that they genuinely cared meant a great deal more to me. Di Giulio (2007) affirms that "caring teachers show their care by building and maintaining a person-to-person relationship with their students" (p. 37). These teachers knew my strengths and helped me accelerate my progress in those areas.

Influence is powerful, but influence is only available if a relationship exists. The elementary teacher and English teacher I mentioned had influence with me precisely because they took the time to get to know me and develop that relationship over time. They accelerated my pace as a voracious reader and writer by encouraging me at every turn. I even learned to love grammar (Imagine that!) in their classrooms. Their knowledge of content was equal to and superseded by their understanding of the importance of building relationships.

Teach People First

In our headlong rush to cover the material for an increasing number of mandated assessments, teachers and administrators need to consider the long-term effects of sacrificing relationship building on the altar of course content. Saying that we teach people—not content—does not diminish the importance of the content, but it does put it in perspective. Tomlinson and Jarvis (2006) capture exactly the balance necessary for students to succeed: "Good teaching is inevitably the fine art of connecting content and kids—of doing what it takes to adapt *how* we teach so that *what* we teach takes hold in the lives and minds of students" (pp. 16–17). Tomlinson and Jarvis emphasize the importance of teaching to the strengths of students *after putting in the time necessary to recognize those strengths*. Those teachers from my youth who made a lasting impression on me recognized my strengths and helped nurture them. Teachers who take the time to discover what is *inside* their students are making deposits in the relationship bank.

After observing and surveying middle school students, Bosworth (1995) concluded that "young adolescents see caring demonstrated within the context of personal relationships." Caring behaviors are also seen not as "a single general act, [but] in the context of an ongoing relationship" (p. 692). Teachers, according to Bosworth, not only need to work on modeling caring behaviors but also need to provide opportunities for students to do that as well (p. 693). The responsibility for initiating the relationship-building process in the classroom rests squarely with the teacher. Relationships established well and early need to be sustained over time.

For the past fifteen years, I have observed teachers at all grade levels. In cases where discipline was not a problem and where students were engaged and attentive, it was obvious that those teachers had taken the time to foster positive personal relationships. Those teachers were calm, comfortable, and caring. On the other hand, in classes where discipline was a constant problem and students were engaged in everything *but* the lesson, it was just as obvious that little time had gone into developing ongoing positive relationships. According to Marzano (2003b), "An effective relationship may be the keystone that allows the other aspects to work well. If a teacher has a good relationship with students, then students accept her rules, procedures, and disciplinary actions" (p. 91). Neglecting to build strong relationships with students will prove costly in the long run for students and teachers alike.

One of the things we ask students to do on a daily basis is to take risks. Speaking in front of classmates involves taking a considerable risk if the student feels that the teacher may react negatively or fail to squelch any negative remarks from other students. The *trust* that is the foundation of any personal relationship plays an important role in teacher-student interactions and in the student's willingness to step outside his comfort zone in the interest of learning. A classroom where negative relationships abound will engender fear and stress "that will block our most well-intended instructional objectives" (Bluestein, 2001, p. 32). A classroom where the teacher models positive, supportive behaviors and insists that her students do likewise should be relatively free of stress.

I have observed classrooms where teachers ask students to do something (or stop doing something) by saying, "I want you to . . ." or "I wish you would . . . ." In classrooms where positive teacher-student relationships are nonexistent, the use of these "I messages" is ineffective at best and inflammatory at worst. Grinder (2006) explains that "positions of authority can only effectively use 'I' when there is a relationship between the sender and the receiver" (p. 113). Substitute teachers learn very quickly what kind of teacher-student relationships exist when they bring up the teacher's name in class. A substitute teacher who says, "I will tell the teacher of your behavior!" in a classroom where relationship building has been ignored by the regular teacher may find that the comment actually worsens the behavior of the students.

Building positive relationships with students is made more difficult if teachers model inappropriate behavior. For example, teachers who publicly criticize students on a regular basis undermine the relationships they should be trying to build. Teachers who should be—but aren't—attempting to construct solid foundational relationships with and among students may actually become the enemy in the eyes of the kids (Good & Brophy, 1984, p. 153). The way one student is treated by the teacher is not lost on the others in the classroom, whether that treatment is helpful or destructive. Teachers must take into account the group dynamics at work in a classroom of thirty kids. Grinder (2006) asserts that a healthy classroom "can only occur when group dynamics are the foundation of management" (p. 1). I remember observing a teacher who broke her own classroom rules regularly during the thirty minutes I was in the classroom. It was painfully obvious that the teacher was modeling the exact opposite of what she was expecting from her students. Teachers who do not model appropriate behavior can expect students to do likewise. What the teacher *does* will trump what the teacher *says* every time.

Building Trust and a Collaborative Culture

Amy is a veteran student who is now in the tenth grade. In a new science classroom in September, she begins to intuit what the group dynamics will be under the direction of this new and unknown teacher. Will he allow students to be sarcastic in class? Will he keep his word? Will he lose his temper and, if so, will this happen frequently? How will he react when her friend Josh loses his temper, which Josh is almost certain to do? Will the teacher show Amy and her classmates the respect that is number one on his posted list of rules? Will he hold himself and his students accountable? Amy does not like public praise and wonders if this teacher will take the time during the first week of school to find out who does and does not like being praised in front of the class. As Amy listens to him welcome everyone to this fifth-period class, all these thoughts run through her mind, and not for the first time in her long career as a student. The answers to those questions will go a long way toward telling Amy what the year will be like in this high school classroom.

Any action on the part of the teacher is not lost on her students. As we saw in the story of Mrs. Randall at the beginning of Chapter 1, a teacher who loses her temper with a student affects the way the entire room full of students views her when the tantrum is over. Grinder (2006) reminds us that managing an individual student has a direct impact on "how the class will view the teacher after the management is done" (p. 3). Kids who feel thankful not to have been on the short end of the teacher's wrath this time will consider that it could be them next time. This sort of "duck-in-a-shooting-gallery" mentality is not likely to build the level of trust necessary for the development of a safe classroom culture. Sitting anxiously, waiting for the boom to be lowered by a teacher who is prone to reactive discipline is not conducive to learning.

Charles and Charles (2004) suggest that one way to build trust is "to interact with students on the principles of kindness, consideration, helpfulness, fairness, and honesty" (p. 45) and to conduct class meetings where those five principles are discussed. Teachers should emphasize that these principles are important not only in teacher-student relationships but in those between students in the classroom. A teacher who does not personally use sarcasm yet allows students to use it is going to find that this adversely affects the classroom environment. The teacher who yells at two students because they just yelled at each other is likewise in for trouble. Whatever principles guide behavior and collaboration in the classroom must apply to students and teachers alike.

The culture of the classroom will either foster learning or make learning difficult. Teachers who simply rely on their authority to get the job done may find the going rough. Goodlad (2004) found that student perceptions are critical.

> In our data, whether or not teachers were perceived to be concerned about students appeared to be significantly related to student satisfaction with their classes. We found that students in classes where teachers were judged to be authoritarian were likely to feel less satisfied. (p. 111)

Whether the going is easy or hard in a classroom is closely tied to a caring attitude and the ability to forge strong, positive relationships with students.

Teachers have a formidable, yet necessary task when it comes to creating a classroom where care, trust, respect, and consistently positive interrelationships are the order of the day—and where fear and stress have been diminished or eliminated completely. Time is of the essence in education, and resistance on the part of students can make learning difficult, if not impossible. On the other hand, in the words of Boynton and Boynton (2005), "When students feel that you value and care for them as individuals, they are more willing to comply with your wishes" (p. 6). Teaching in a classroom where students are willing participants is a much more desirable prospect (and infinitely less costly) than trying to drag unwilling kids kicking and screaming into the content.

Before creating a nurturing and safe climate in the classroom, teachers need to understand that establishing solid and successful relationships with students is not a solo act. "Teachers in today's society cannot handle all situations on their own; they need to learn to collaborate with administrators, with special needs educators, and with their students' parents" (Witmer, 2005, p. 225). This also means that building and district administrators need to place a greater emphasis on establishing effective and lasting relationships within the school community. Teachers need to make certain their classroom rules and consequences are in line with building policy so that there is not a disconnect.

Bluestein (1999) reminds us that "because teaching is an interactive experience, a positive teacher-student relationship increases the likelihood that the time students and teachers spend together will be more effective and enjoyable for all concerned" (p. 35). If building positive and productive relationships is critical to school success, then what can educators do to lay the foundation for that success? For one thing, they can discover the role and the power of listening in communicating.

Developing Listening Skills

In my undergraduate days, I had a speech course in which I learned to make speeches that demonstrated and persuaded. Yet not once did I encounter any courses on listening. This is, by and large, true of our K–12 system of education. "We spend 55 percent of our lives listening," says Costa (2008), "yet it is one of the least taught skills in schools" (p. 33). If we are to understand the kids we teach, then it follows that we need to do more listening and learn how to do it well. Moreover, if understanding our kids' parents is important, then it is necessary that we *listen* to parents.

During the course of any given school year, opportunities arise where teachers need the support of parents. Even though we as educators know in advance that the moment will come, we often neglect to make the early phone calls that establish teacher-parent relationships. Getting insights from parents can help teachers unravel a mystery or solve a problem and, at the same time, demonstrate to the parent that this is a teacher who listens. Evans (2004) puts it this way: "Listening to parents is vital for gaining information, for conveying interest and empathy, and for building and sustaining cooperative relationships. Plus, the principles of good listening lead naturally into the principles of good telling when it is the teacher's turn to talk" (p. 211).

Evans (2004) also reminds us that teachers worry about how they will *deliver* a particular message to parents. It never occurred to me as a new teacher that my job was to *listen* to parents and empathize with their point of view, all the while "checking and clarifying to be sure you've understood them by restating what you've heard" (p. 211). Everyone has been involved as the speaker in a conversation where it seems quite clear that the listener is not listening. "We often say we are listening, but in actuality we are rehearsing in our head what we are going to say next when our partner is finished" (Costa, 2008, p. 33). The teacher who simply unloads on a parent in an attempt to *get the message across* and *get off the phone* is making an expensive mistake. Staying calm, listening empathetically, and working with a parent to resolve a problem may take longer, but it is worth the time spent by both parties.

Timing is also critical. My own experience as a teacher taught me early on that gaining the cooperation and respect of my students' parents began in August, not September. As soon as class lists are available, teachers can begin making phone calls every day prior to the start of school. For me, those early investments in relationship building with parents paid off later in the year if I had to make the phone calls that were uncomfortable because the message was less than positive. If *that* phone call is essentially one in which the parent is somewhat taken by surprise and is on the defensive, then the conversation may indeed be difficult for both parties. Teachers need to make the positive calls before having to make more difficult calls later in the year. If you are already on firm footing with parents, those calls may be less uncomfortable—and they will most certainly be more productive.

August is also the time to find out from parents what their children enjoy doing and where their academic strengths and weaknesses may lie. This is critical because knowing these things early gives teachers an advantage in those critical first weeks of school. While teachers will certainly want to help students deal with their weak academic subjects, knowing their talents and strengths will help teachers accelerate growth in those areas. Gordon (2006) says that while research on talent-based development continues, "the preponderance of evidence thus far is that performance improves most, and most rapidly, when the developmental focus is on strengths rather than on remediation of weaknesses" (p. 112). The teacher who knows at the beginning of school which students have particular areas of strength is in a position to facilitate further growth right out of the gate.

During those early conversations, teachers can find out which parents are willing to help and get involved with field trips, projects, and tutoring. Gathering this information before school begins will help later on when knowing which parent will help with what activity or event may become important. I have found that talking to a parent with whom you have already established a working relationship pays big dividends in any number of ways throughout the entire school year. This is another case of investing up front for a subsequent payoff.

While there is much parents can do, there are things teachers should discourage. Di Giulio (2007) cautions against asking parents to "punish children for school behavior" (p. 79). Such a request may, in some cases, lead to abuse. Di Giulio states that even if the expectation is that the parent(s) cannot do much to correct—from home—a misbehavior at school, "parental awareness of the problem and their wish to cooperate are vital to your management plan. Involve parents early, and be prepared to outline your ideas. They will look to you for specific action because they already know all too well about their child's misbehavior" (p. 79).

My suggestion is that new teachers sit down with administrators and find out which teachers in the building have the best reputation for building strong relationships. Then, call those teachers and offer to take them to lunch! Even an hour or two with a highly effective veteran will give new teachers strategies for considerable success throughout the school year.

Also, teachers would do well to commit to doing more listening than talking during the course of the school year, not just in August. Learn to listen to colleagues, students, and parents in such a way that your mind is not working on what you will say next. The teacher who sends the message that she is not really listening may find the favor returned. Someone once commented that since we have two ears and only one mouth, that should cue us in as to the relative importance of the art of listening.

Improving Teacher-to-Student and Student-to-Student Communication

Students are nothing if not perceptive. They are all-seeing and all-knowing when it comes to the dynamics of the classroom. From the time they walk into a teacher's classroom for the first time, students are using higher-order thinking skills. They are comparing and contrasting this new teacher with one from the past. They are inferring, based on available evidence (as Amy did earlier in this chapter), what this teacher might do given a particular set of circumstances. They are studying the "facial expressions, tone of voice, body language, and comments that emanate from their teachers" (Brown, 2005, p. 15). Nothing escapes their notice, and they will make important decisions about how engaged they will become (and about how they will behave!) based on the data they collect and analyze.

One important piece of data to which students pay a good deal of attention is body language—specifically the gap between what the teacher *vocalizes* and what his body *communicates*. Charles (2002) affirms that if there is a significant gap between what the teacher *said* and what the student *observed*, "the body message carries the stronger impact" (p. 83). Teachers would do well to eliminate gestures, facial expressions, and other forms of body language that form barriers to communication. For example, a teacher who listens to a student with his arms crossed and a scowl on his face is sending a negative message without saying a word.

One of the most effective and successful presenters I know speaks with a modicum of hand gestures and listens in a fully supportive position with his hands at his sides, facing the seminar participant who has just asked a question or raised an issue. His focused listening supports the contention that listening is an active and not a passive process. Before answering a question, he pauses to think and takes the time to clarify what the participant meant before providing an answer. His words are all the more effective because they are not discounted by negative body language. His body language fully supports his verbal message, and he seeks clarity and understanding at every turn. These are skills to be emulated by teachers and taught to students.

Communication is a two-way street. The first week of school is a great time to work with students on their speaking and listening skills. Teachers should provide gobs of opportunities for students to meet in pairs (sitting and standing) and have structured conversations where they can practice listening actively and avoiding the kind of negative body language that can destroy a conversation quickly. Students who develop a habit of listening with their arms crossed, looking at the clock or their watches, or offering scowls or looks of disbelief are going to find student-to-student conversations difficult, if not impossible. A student who reads his conversation partner's body language or facial expressions and comes to the conclusion that there is no sense in continuing will simply shut down. The likelihood that there will be no return on investment will more often than not short circuit the conversation before it begins. *Students must be taught that speaking and listening are two sides of the same conversational coin.*

Any teacher looking to build solid and lasting relationships in the classroom should understand that effective communication is both cause and effect. When students learn to communicate effectively, respect the opinions of others in that communication, and communicate openly and honestly, relationships can prosper. The teacher who labors to build relationships that are open, honest, and built on trust will find that positive and effective communication will help keep it cheap in terms of a smooth-running classroom.

Forging and Sustaining Adult Relationships

In a later chapter, we will deal with collaboration as it relates to instruction, but we can hardly talk about relationships without spending some time on those between and among staff members in the school community.

If teachers need to focus on their students, it follows that building administrators should focus on teachers. Sergiovanni (2005) reminds us that "All of the learning and all of the support we want students to experience depends in large measure on the support that teachers receive" (p. 101). Sergiovanni adds, "An important truism is that as the principal goes, so goes the school. But the corollary to that statement is also true. As the teacher goes, so goes the student" (p. 101). Students and teachers alike are nothing if not perceptive. My experience has been that students take their lead from their teachers every bit as much as teachers take their lead from administrators. The culture of the classroom cannot help but be affected by the culture of the building as demonstrated by the adults that students observe and with whom they interact every day.

The authoritarian administrator will likely have the same negative effect on the staff that the authoritarian teacher has on the students. I have heard many teachers say, "Just tell me what you want to do!" and in the next breath complain because they can't do what they themselves recognize needs to be done. I have also seen many of those same teachers, seemingly on the motivational "critical list," revive when allowed to participate in the decisions, innovations, and problem solving as part of a truly collaborative school culture. I have seen people I thought were diehard cynics become actively involved in genuine, collaborative, leadership-driven efforts at improving the way things are because for the first time in their careers they have a voice and because they believe administrators value their input.

Roland Barth (2001), looking back on his experience as a teacher and principal, said he "learned over and over again that the relationship among the adults in the schoolhouse has more impact on the quality and the character of the school—and on the accomplishments of youngsters—than any other factor" (p. 105).

> I have found no characteristic of a good school more pervasive than healthy teacher-principal relationships—and no characteristic of a troubled school more common than troubled, embattled, or antiseptic administrator-teacher relationships. (p. 105)

Veteran teachers at any level in the educational system, public or private, know full well that adult relationships in the building will set the tone for adult-student relationships. A teacher who looks forward to coming to school every day because the school culture is positive is likely to pass that forward to the kids in her care.

According to Blankstein (2004), "Relationships support a leader in taking the risk to act from his or her *core* to create *organizational meaning*. Relationships allow leaders to maintain *clarity and constancy of purpose* and to *face the data and the fears*, though this might otherwise be too stressful, threatening, and disheartening" (p. 28). This means that building administrators need to take the first step in building leadership capacity by taking the time to "make room in conversations, dialogues, and meetings for others to give voice to their concerns about working relationships and to celebrate their productive collaborations" (Donaldson, 2001, p. 57).

Not paying attention, then, to building and nurturing adult relationships is likely to prove extremely expensive to all concerned. On the other hand, a building in which teachers regularly seek the opinions of other teachers and work together to create a positive atmosphere is likely a place students will want to attend. It is also a place where teachers will happily spend many years as part of an extended family dedicated to the kids in its care.

Final Thoughts

In Chapter 1, we emphasized the importance of making procedures routine, properly positioning process before content in the scheme of things. To this we have now added the building of relationships with students, parents, and colleagues. This foundation of smooth-running processes and solid relationships will do much to ensure success over time. Students who feel at home in a smoothly functioning classroom where the teacher takes the time to develop and foster positive relationships are far more likely to experience success. This does not happen by chance but by deliberate and reflective planning in the weeks and months leading up to a new school year. According to Bluestein (1999), "Working to build a positive classroom climate— even if temporarily at the expense of the curriculum—can help us avoid being sabotaged by negative attitudes, weak learning behaviors and unrealistic self-expectations as well" (p. 35).

In Chapter 3, we'll look closely at something directly related to building relationships and creating a safe classroom environment— self-control on the part of the teacher. We'll discover that keeping it cheap means avoiding losing one's temper—a reaction that can, at least temporarily, derail the learning process and threaten the very relationships teachers may otherwise be working hard to build.

3

Getting a Handle on Self-Control

A good friend of mine is a substitute teacher at the high school level. She is one of the most consistently positive and articulate human beings I have had the good fortune to meet over the years. She is also an excellent substitute teacher, in part because she understands the importance of remaining calm in the face of rude or unruly students. A female high school student once stood toe to toe with her and let loose a torrent of verbal abuse that would have gotten a strong reaction from many, perhaps most, teachers. She simply stood there with her hands at her sides and let the girl run out of steam. After a couple of minutes, having finally run out of things to say, the student walked back to her seat and sat down, apparently exhausted by the effort. This substitute teacher, who had never said a word during the entire tirade, called one of the security assistants and wrote up the incident on a discipline referral slip. She then continued with the class.

In observing teachers over the years, I have found a common thread that runs through the classrooms of those who are most effective. Like the substitute teacher in the story above, those teachers are habitually calm and possess a great deal of self-confidence. Discipline problems, where they exist, are handled firmly, quietly, and without disrupting the flow of process in the classroom. Things in the best classrooms get done efficiently, and students are too busily engaged in the learning process to misbehave. In the most effective classrooms, respect is not just a word on a laminated wall chart. Respect is tangible and it is mutual. Teachers in those classrooms are consistently in control of their own actions and reactions.

In other classrooms I have observed, it is clear that teachers are simply not in control of their own emotions or actions. These teachers spend an inordinate amount of time reacting to unruly students and to situations that arise because students have little respect for the teacher or for their own classmates. In this kind of chaotic environment, learning takes place in fits and starts and often takes a back seat to classroom disruptions, dissonance, and discord. Procedures appear to be nonexistent, laminated posters containing classroom rules are ignored, and the only consequences in evidence are negative and unintended; teaching and learning are casualties of an unmanaged and unsafe environment.

Several years ago, in a three-day classroom management seminar taught by Fred Jones, Dr. Jones used the example of baseball umpires to illustrate the choice between staying in control of oneself and handing control over to someone else. As I thought back to my childhood, it occurred to me that some of my fondest memories are of summer trips to Cleveland to see a baseball doubleheader between the Cleveland Indians and the New York Yankees, or some other American League team. On occasion, a good deal of entertainment was provided by irate managers or ballplayers whose verbal targets were almost always umpires. In fact, I often thought that umpires must love what they do, because the fairly frequent abuse they take would leave most human beings drained and in search of another profession. Some umpires responded verbally and met the verbal onslaught decibel for decibel and gesture for gesture. Some of those confrontations would go on forever, with the crowd adding to the din . . . tens of thousands of people shouting insults at the unfortunate umpire or, if his antagonist was from the other team, the other team's manager.

Occasionally, there was an umpire who refused to get upset. He would simply stand there, facing his antagonist, without saying a word. The manager would attempt an escalation by throwing his hat on the ground or kicking dirt around, first with one foot and then with the other. The umpire would just stand there, and I often wondered what he was thinking. Finally, the manager, unable to provoke a response and realizing his tirade was getting him nowhere, would grab his hat and simply walk away, muttering to himself. The umpire would then clean off home plate and go back to work.

In both examples, the umpire and the substitute teacher mentioned at the beginning of this chapter realized that getting upset would accomplish nothing constructive and might well add fuel to the fire. For their part, once the angry baseball manager and the verbally abusive high school student finally realized there was nothing to be gained by continuing to fuss and fume, they simply walked away.

Shouting at students in a fit of anger is part of what Bluestein (1999) calls a power-based and control-oriented approach. If a teacher is looking for short-term compliance from most students, she may accomplish that with an angry tirade, but this choice will be extremely expensive in at least four ways. First, it will negatively affect the quality of the relationship between the student and the teacher (Bluestein, 1999, p. 39). Second, the way in which a teacher treats a given student *does not go unnoticed* by the rest of the students in the class. According to Grinder (2006), in the early stages of class formation, "how the teacher treats each student is how the rest of the class believes they will be treated" (p. 34). Third, aggressive behavior on the part of the teacher can trigger aggressiveness on the part of the students, especially if the students read the teacher's outburst as an attack (Bailey, 2000, pp. 106–107). Finally, when a teacher loses her temper, it sends the message that losing one's temper is perfectly acceptable behavior when confronted by someone who won't do what we want them to do. Teachers who repeatedly lash out at students will have a hard time making the case that students should not respond in kind. Once again, modeling appropriate behavior is a good, inexpensive way to invest in appropriate student behavior throughout the year.

Getting upset at a student or at the class is costly in another way. Teachers may absolve themselves of responsibility for the outburst and instead choose to blame the students. According to Bailey, however, "If you believe the children are *making you* scream at them, you have placed them in charge of you" (p. 28). While it is true that the students may have *triggered* the upset, it is the teacher who *caused* it (p. 29).

Tate (2007) gives teachers a wonderful simile that puts into perspective the tremendous cost of losing one's temper in the classroom: "It has been said that shouting to manage students is like blowing the horn to steer a car. After all, excessive blowing of horns escalates road rage just like excessive shouting at students escalates power struggles" (pp. xvi–xvii). Teachers should work to help students display the kind of self-control that makes these blowups less likely, says Feinstein (2004), and using these "positive discipline strategies will defuse most potential explosions; when it doesn't, staying calm and acting decisively will help cool tempers down" (p. 90).

Finally, a teacher who lashes out at a student or at the whole class runs the risk of raising his or her own stress level significantly. A rise in stress levels triggers a significant release of cortisol, a hormone necessary for helping the body deal with emergencies. Over time, high levels of cortisol can impair health (Goleman, 2006; Wolfe, 2001). Maintaining a calm, emotionally-safe classroom environment is important to building relationships and, ultimately, to learning. The expense of an emotionally dysfunctional classroom is borne not just by students, but by teachers as well. Teachers who must continually rely on the use of power to control students will likely not be happy in their profession and may become victims of burnout.

Displaying and Maintaining Consistently Calm Behavior

Some teachers are, by nature, calm and unruffled under any circumstances. Others may have to work at the kind of self-discipline that will keep them from losing their temper and creating an unsafe atmosphere in the classroom. If losing one's temper is too expensive, let's discover how to cut costs. Below are some suggestions for maintaining the kind of consistent behavior that will serve as a model to the students.

1. When a student does something inappropriate and you determine you are going to have to say or do something, *avoid a knee-jerk reaction that may get you in trouble.* Goleman (1995) calls this a *neural hijacking* where, having perceived an immediate threat, "a center in the limbic brain proclaims an emergency, recruiting the rest of the brain to its urgent agenda." This happens in the critical moments "before the neocortex, the thinking brain, has had a chance to glimpse fully what is happening, let alone decide if it is a good idea" (p. 14). If someone is in true danger or under attack, this reaction is eminently useful. If, however, this hijacking is triggered by the actions of a student doing something that simply angers us, it can be tremendously expensive. Overreacting can lead to an escalation that can quickly spiral out of control. On the other hand, pausing, taking a

couple of deep breaths, or even counting to ten while you thoughtfully consider what you are going to say or do next in a crisis, are all powerful tools (Tate, 2007, p. 4).

2. Jones (2007) points out that when a teacher sees disruptive behavior in the classroom, she or he will "have a fight-flight reflex" that cannot be prevented, but can be overridden with a learned response—*relaxation* (p. 180). This involves relaxed breathing and a conscious effort to stay calm. According to Jones (2007),

> A relaxing breath is slow and relatively shallow. It is the way you would breathe if you were watching television or reading a magazine. It lowers your heart rate and your blood pressure. Your muscles relax, and your face becomes calm and expressionless. (p. 181)

3. If you need to speak to a student or to the whole class about something related to discipline, move away from the board (or wherever you are at the moment) to another place in the room, even if it is only a few feet away, before saying anything. It gives you a chance to breathe and think; this repositioning sends a signal that you are about to switch from teaching mode to discipline mode. When you have said what you need to say, move back to the original position as a visual signal that you are moving back into instruction mode.

4. From the beginning of the school year, invest a great deal of energy in building positive and trust-centered relationships with your students and their parents. As we saw in Chapter 2, making a series of phone calls to the parents or visiting the homes of your students before school even starts sends a message that you are willing to invest your own time in building relationships. An investment like this up front will pay off later if there is a problem with a student that requires a conversation with someone at home. Most people, for example, are far less likely to fly off the handle at someone with whom they have built a solid relationship. Those positive relationships will make the occasions when tempers explode much less frequent.

5. If you find that you need to have a serious conversation with a student, avoid doing it publicly. My own observation of classrooms over the years has proved again and again the efficacy of private conversations done in a quiet corner of the room, just outside the door in the hallway, or after class. Students who

like to "perform" find they have no audience in a one-on-one conversation conducted in measured tones. Later on, after making this time investment, a mere look on the part of the teacher may easily redirect misbehavior on the part of the student.

6. If you find it necessary to have a conversation with a parent on the telephone, don't call while you are upset over something that just happened. The anger generated by your reaction to what happened may lead to your saying something you will later regret. The same applies in this age of e-mail, and e-mails are forever. Think through what you will say to the parent and resolve to *listen* as well as to talk. These occasions, as we have seen, are made easier by having established a relationship with the parent early on.

7. Spend some time during staff meetings exploring strategies for reducing the kind of verbal confrontations that compromise the efficacy of the school's mission. Discuss with your colleagues ways to improve the emotional environment of the school both in the classroom and in other areas of the building and grounds. This reduces the number of times students will come into your classroom having been upset and highly stressed in the previous period or classroom. My sense is that the entire faculty can benefit from a collective decision to reduce the global expense of classrooms that are emotionally unsafe. Administrators can facilitate this whole process by providing time during faculty meetings to discuss ways to create a safe climate in the building.

8. If you have an iPod or other MP3 player, identify your thirty or forty favorite songs and put them in a special file called *Getting Ready* or *Setup*. While you are driving to work, or once you get into your classroom, play those songs as you prepare for the school day. Music has the power to shift (and lift) a mood in a hurry. If you play songs that have positive emotional attachments from your life, this will help get you ready for the day ahead. If you play music for the students as they come into the room, it will help set them up for the day as well. Emotions are contagious, and your students deserve a teacher that is calm, upbeat, and ready to help them face the school day.

9. Give yourself some time during the day when you can disconnect for a short time. Rick Smith (2004), when he was teaching, experimented with the time between classes:

> When the bell would ring to signal break, after the kids had flown out of the room, I would do nothing. I would simply stand still, and begin to notice my feet—I tend to forget I have feet when I am teaching. I might stand still, I might walk slowly around the room, I might take my shoes off. Slowly I'd begin to notice my breath. What part of my body was receiving breath? I might walk over to the window and look out at the trees to the right, not at the traffic to the left, and maybe gaze at the bird's nests that had been built in the corner of my windows. (p. 47)

What Smith did *not* do was anything related to teaching (grading tests or returning phone calls, for example). He considered that short break his time and his alone. I would have called the exercise "recharging my batteries," and for me it often involved playing some music between classes.

Appropriate humor can be an effective tool for handling potentially difficult situations. Peter Johnston, author of *Choice Words: How Our Language Affects Children's Learning* (2004), tells the story of his fourth-grade teacher who, responding to one of the young Johnston's transgressions said, "By the gods, thou art a scurvy knave. Verily I shall bonce thee on thine evil sconce." It got Johnston's attention immediately and had the desired effect. His teacher's intriguing use of language and humor showed Johnston "how valuable and interesting language can be—valuable enough to play with, powerful enough to change behavior without force" (p. 1).

Investing time up front in planning, building relationships, and committing to staying cool, calm, and collected is a great way to keep it cheap later on.

Transfer of Ownership

I suggest that teachers use some time periodically to discuss with students the importance of a healthy classroom environment, along with how they (and the teacher) can contribute to that environment at every turn. Questions can be posted and can serve as the basis for a discussion on how things have been going. For example, were there occasions during the course of the week when the failure to remain calm (on anyone's part) affected the classroom environment? Were there times when someone was initially angered but then paused, took a couple of deep breaths, and by so doing avoided confrontation?

Are there things that students *can do or avoid doing* that will contribute to a healthy climate and help avoid expensive missteps later on?

Kids are incredibly perceptive, as we have seen, and they are eager to help solve problems related to what is going on in the classroom *if we seek their input and their assistance.* Using their feedback on a weekly basis, teachers can improve process in the classroom. Students need to know that "their actions can make a difference in what happens" (Curwin, 2003, p. 15). Frequent conversations about the need for responsibility on the part of students may well lead to fewer disruptions and, as a result, fewer occasions when a teacher comes face to face with losing control.

For those considering this effort at collective progress and continuous improvement, the age of the students is, I believe, largely irrelevant. I once observed a kindergarten teacher brainstorming with her students what went well on a recent field trip and what they could all do together (teacher and students) to improve their next foray into the community—a trip to the zoo. By being proactive and leading her kids in a discussion of what might happen to derail the next field trip, that kindergarten teacher increased her percentage of success and decreased the number of occasions where being reactive could lead to her losing her self-control while at the zoo.

I know an eighth-grade teacher who became increasingly aware as the school year progressed that the amount of homework being turned in by his students was steadily declining. In his frustration, this teacher could have played the blame game and lost his temper in front of the class, assuming that his students had to be at fault. Instead, he took the time to brainstorm with the class reasons why the situation was deteriorating week after week. Working as a group, the class identified several reasons for the steady decline and then they all (teacher and students) worked together to find solutions to the agreed-on root causes. Process had triumphed over emotion and, as a consequence, the problem was solved.

Teachers who lose their self-control while angrily reminding thirty students of their collective shortcomings are, in my experience, doomed to fail. Playing the blame game in this way is seldom productive and is likely to lead to increased resentment on the part of the students. Also, when a teacher gets visibly upset by things that (invariably) happen in the classroom, the learning process is derailed for a period of time. Teachers would do well, according to Costa (2008), to "try to restrain their impulsivity by avoiding strong emotional reactions to classroom events, since emotions tend to preempt attention" (p. 180). The costs associated with even a momentary loss of self-control on the part of a teacher can be steep. Those costs include a loss of respect, trust, and, according to Hannaford (2005), "decreased learning and memory" due to the increased cortisol levels that occur when students are stressed (p. 178). Constantly practicing strategies for remaining calm in the face of adversity will pay big dividends down the road.

In Chapter 1, we emphasized the role well-rehearsed procedures play in creating a smoothly functioning classroom. In Chapter 2, we moved from procedures and rules into the realm of building relationships with students and between and among students in classrooms. Tempers tend to flare when students do not feel safe, when ambiguity breeds uncertainty as related to classroom rules, and when teachers are inconsistent in their dealings with students. The teachers who constantly find themselves reacting to events in the classroom because they did not take the time to frontload in the area of process will pay a steep price, as will their students. Taking the time to "think ahead sufficiently to foresee potential problems," according to Charles and Charles (2004, p. 145) is necessary, especially when "students sometimes do and say things intentionally to get under your skin, hoping to see you become upset and befuddled and, perhaps, lose self-control" (p. 145).

Final Thoughts

We know a good deal today about how the brain functions as it relates to human emotions and learning. Teachers should learn all they can about how the brain does what it does *and then share it with the students.* If the business of learning includes how we remember things, why not share that with them? Discuss with students the role of neurotransmitters like serotonin and dopamine in the learning process. Explain the function of cortisol to students, as well as the term *neural hijacking* so they understand what, physiologically, causes us to react negatively in an instant, only to regret it later on. Talk with them frankly about the costs associated with losing one's temper and the concomitant benefits of staying in control.

For their part, administrators can use time set aside for professional development to involve the *entire staff* in learning as much as possible about how the brain functions as it relates to learning and why it is important for everyone in the schoolhouse to model the kind of behavior we want our kids to emulate. Once again, time invested up front will help keep it cheap for everyone concerned when situations surface that underline the importance of maintaining self-control and the costs associated with losing it.

In Chapter 4, we'll look at ways to engage students in their own learning and reduce the amount of time they spend as passive observers. Someone once said that too many kids come to school to watch their teachers work; this, to the extent it is true, needs to be changed. If teachers are doing the work and students are not engaged, it is too expensive for everyone concerned. Engagement on the part of students leads to understanding and retention. Additionally, students who are not engaged in the learning process may find other outlets for their desire to *do* something, and this can become too expensive for the teacher. Keep it cheap.

4

Shifting Students From Passive to Active

One particular active-classroom success story involves two fifth-grade teachers who taught as a team at the elementary level and whose classrooms were across the hall from each other. Cindy Rickert (social studies and language arts) and Emma Jeter (math and science) replaced student desks with four-person tables that they placed around the perimeter of the classroom. This had the effect of opening up the middle of both rooms in order to facilitate movement. Emma painted a number grid on the floor of her classroom where students could actively practice their multiplication tables while moving from square to square on the grid. Cindy created a hopscotch-like design of letters on her classroom floor so students could practice spelling by jumping from letter to letter. In both classrooms, movement, conversation, and collaboration were the order of the day.

What resulted from their efforts that first year of utilizing the active classroom concepts was that the kids loved coming to school in the morning, their grades (both within the classroom and on division and state tests) improved tremendously, the kids' parents enthusiastically supported the program, and two things disappeared: worksheets and discipline referrals. Those forty-eight fifth graders became a family, and at the open house the following year, Cindy and Emma brought back one of their students from the previous school year to help explain to the parents what active learning can accomplish.

My experience is that the most resourceful students at any grade level are quite adept at finding reasons to get up and move during class. Getting permission to make a trip to the restroom, going to the pencil sharpener, or volunteering to erase the board (without being asked) are a few of the strategies kids use to keep from sitting for extended periods of time. I have observed that adults don't like to sit still for more than a few minutes either. As a middle school and high school teacher, I was on my feet most of the time. Thinking back, I had a definite advantage over my students because standing and moving were all part of my repertoire. I did my lecturing standing up, and the students did their part by sitting quietly and taking notes . . . for the better part of an hour.

Goodlad (2004) and his team of researchers observed more than one thousand classrooms at all levels. The subsequent data supported "the popular image of a teacher standing or sitting in front of a class imparting knowledge to a group of students" (p. 105). Teacher talk dominated, and they observed "a low incidence of activities invoking active modes of learning" (p. 105). In one hallway of a junior high school, Goodlad looked into the open doorways of three classrooms and observed that, while the teachers sat at their own desks, students sat in rows. "Most were writing, a few were stretching, and the remainder were looking contemplatively or blankly into space" (p. 93). One could easily draw the conclusion that those students were not deeply involved in course content.

Learning and memory may not be best served by sitting and contemplating for extended periods of time. In fact, as Hannaford (2005) asserts, learning and memory are clearly linked to movement. "Movement awakens and activates many of our mental capacities. Movement integrates and anchors new information and experience into our neural networks" (p. 107). According to Jensen (2005), "Evidence from imaging sources, anatomical studies, and clinical data shows that moderate exercise enhances cognitive processing" (p. 67). If movement is clearly linked to learning and memory, then teachers need to integrate movement into their planning.

The evidence is not all clinical, and simple observation over time can tell us much about the effect of sitting still for any length of time. I had occasion years ago to pass by a college classroom several times in the course of a class session. The method of instructional delivery was lecture, and each time I passed by the classroom, I noticed more and more students in various modes of disengagement. By the fourth or fifth pass, several were asleep with their heads on the tables. The instructor continued to talk, seemingly unaffected by the students' inattention.

Kids Gotta Move

Any parent knows that kids have to move and that kids (and adults) do not enjoy sitting still for long periods of time. In spite of the evidence that spending a good deal of any class period in a sitting position does not enhance learning, lecture and seatwork continue to predominate, especially at the middle school and high school levels. If time is a precious (and scarce) commodity in the classroom, then these passive modes of instruction are too expensive; teachers are working too hard and students are not engaged in their own learning.

McCombs and Whisler (1997) explain that "in the learner-centered classroom, students are actively involved in their learning. Although students are sometimes found sitting at their tables and reading quietly, they may also be found working in cooperative groups, chatting and animated as they find information, make connections, and make discoveries" (p. 91). This describes exactly the classrooms of Cindy Rickert and Emma Jeter, whose story opened this chapter. Those two teachers took a risk on behalf of their kids and were successful beyond their wildest dreams. They worked incredibly hard getting ready for the lessons, but in the classroom it was the kids who did most of the work. Their initial expenditure of effort and planning made it possible to keep it cheap in the classroom.

For veteran teachers used to shouldering the workload in the classroom, shifting that workload to the students involves, as we saw with Rickert and Jeter, considerable risk. Such a change involves substantial risk on the part of the kids as well. Veteran students may have gotten used to being passive observers and watching the teacher do the work, in which case shifting from passive to active mode may not be easy. Teachers must work with students to get them used to the idea of taking part in student-to-student conversations and collaborating with other students in pairs or in groups on a regular basis.

Fogarty (1990) suggests a gradual move from teachers as lecturers to a more interactive approach where "the students are as active as the teacher," a shift that provides "paradigm shifts for teachers, students, and parents" (p. ix). Cindy Rickert remembers that parents were apprehensive about the new, more active approach until they saw the effect it had on their kids. Not only did they enjoy school more, but their grades (classroom and standardized assessments) improved significantly. It did not take long in that first active-classroom experiment for teachers, students, and parents alike to be sold on its effectiveness.

Facilitating Movement

Neurokinesiologist Jean Blaydes Madigan (2004) points out that "movement, physical activity, and exercise change the learning state into one appropriate for retention and retrieval of memory, the effects lasting as much as 30–60 minutes depending on the student" (p. 15). Getting students up frequently not only gives students a break, then, but it facilitates learning for some time to come after they are seated.

Once teachers commit to a more active classroom, there are a great many ways to increase the opportunities for purposeful and structured movement during a lesson.

1. Every few minutes, simply have the students stand up and stretch or do some basic exercises. This allows them to disconnect from the content for a short time, and they should be ready to go when they return to their seats. One elementary teacher has her third-grade students play musical chairs—without removing a chair—for a minute or so, simply to get them up and get more blood, along with oxygen and glucose, to their brains. Then they return to their seats to the accompaniment of another song.

2. After a mini-lecture, have students stand, find a partner somewhere in the room, and discuss the material. Teachers can circulate, listening to the various conversations and determining the extent to which they have a grasp of the content just covered.

3. While students are taking a test, give them periodic breaks where they can stand, stretch, and take part in some simple exercises. Play some upbeat music and announce that at the end of the song they should sit down and pick up where they left off.

4. Take a close look at the way the classroom is arranged. If the desks are arranged in rows and take up much or most of the available space, it can be difficult for students to move around. Consider using a furniture arrangement that moves the teacher's desk to a corner and opens up space in the middle that will enhance student movement.

5. Before school begins in the morning, take a few minutes to display posters, quotes, math problems, sentences in need of grammatical help, or (in social studies) political cartoons on the walls of the classroom. During class, have students get into groups of three or four and "visit the art gallery." Stephanie Meister, a first-grade teacher in Loudoun County, Virginia, has her students do this at least once per week. Meister said it helped "to develop a sense of community in our classroom as we used it at the very beginning of the year," while later in the year the students used it to "compare and contrast ideas" (S. Meister, personal communication, February 10, 2008).

6. When it is time to distribute handouts or instructions to the students, let them get up and find them somewhere in the room (a treasure hunt) or throw them up into the air and let it "snow" sheets of paper while students scramble to get one. Or give the materials to be distributed to student helpers standing in the four corners of the room. Students can then get their handouts from the helpers—*after paying the helper an appropriate compliment* (Allen, 2002, p. 75). (In one intermediate school, most teachers use this last distribution method and the kids love it. It seems they all want to be the helper . . . and receive the compliments.)

7. Near the end of class, have the students stand in a huge circle and give one of them a soft (safety first!) ball, instructing that student to share aloud one interesting thing learned during the class period. Having thus shared, he throws the ball to someone else and the process is repeated for the available time. This might also be a great time to surface questions students may have about the material just covered. Questions raised can be charted by one of the students. When the ball has made the journey around the circle, students can return to their seats and the questions that were asked and charted can be dealt with.

The purpose of the above activities is to incorporate movement into the lesson; in so doing the teacher provides a break from sitting and an opportunity to allow movement to support learning and memory by improving cognition (Jensen, 2005, p. 60). When planning lessons, teachers can insert plenty of opportunities for movement and structured conversation.

If kids really do resent having to sit still for long periods of time, it is far better that teachers provide the outlet rather than having to react when kids ask to go to the restroom, sharpen their pencils, or otherwise find disruptive ways to move on their own initiative. In short, if the teachers don't make an investment plan for movement, the kids will—and the cost of disruptions is high.

The brain is connected to and affected by physical action and, indeed, "thinking is a response to our physical world" (Hannaford, 2005, p. 120). By integrating movement into daily lessons, teachers enhance learning and memory, and by the way, my experience has been that classroom movement is tremendously enjoyable for teachers and students alike. Getting kids paired up with a partner or formed into small groups is a great way to provide opportunities for reflection and discussion, especially after new information has just been presented during direct instruction. Kaufeldt (2005) asserts that after new information has been introduced, "the learner will need multiple, diverse opportunities to reflect and process" (p. 86). By providing this time for reflective processing, teachers can, according to Kaufeldt, give students an opportunity to

- recall what was just presented,
- orally summarize the lesson,
- listen to someone else's opinion and understanding, and
- be prompted to get their attention back to the lesson (p. 86).

A Commitment to Collaboration

Teachers who make a commitment to creating opportunities for students to share with each other in pairs or in groups will want to work with students to establish what we might call "rules of engagement" so that those conversations can run smoothly. Marzano (2007) recommends that teachers "inform students that they will be working in groups quite frequently" and gives four examples of rules to which students must commit before working collaboratively:

- Be willing to add your perspective to any discussion.
- Respect the opinions of other people.
- Make sure you understand what others have added to the conversation; be willing to ask questions if you don't understand something.
- Be willing to answer questions other group members ask you about your ideas. (p. 44)

Before students can begin to discuss and reflect on content-related information in pairs or in groups, teachers need to take two important steps, both process related:

1. The *first time* students have paired or group conversations, teachers should give them something to talk about that is non-threatening and about which the students know a good deal. For example, I often have students talk about their favorite meal or what jobs they might like to have down the road when they enter the workforce. These are easy topics on which students can elaborate a good deal. (Teachers can model this by describing their own favorite meal or what dreams or goals they have for the future.) This gives students a chance to practice having a discussion without having the added pressure of content-rich material added to the mix. They need to get the process down before they can use the process to tackle content.

2. It is not enough to state or even list the rules of engagement for collaboration. Students need to consciously apply the rules to the conversations until the use of them becomes the norm. While students are getting used to the idea of talking with other students, the teacher should have them practice good listening and paraphrasing skills, along with good questioning techniques. When I have students work in pairs, I have them practice summarizing what their partner says. When students understand that at the end of a period of time they will have to summarize what their partner has explained, they are much more likely to develop good listening habits.

In both cases above, the key is to practice, practice, and practice some more until the rules become embedded in the process and the process is clearly understood by all the students. Only then should content be introduced into the mix. Combining new information with an unfamiliar process will prove too expensive. Teachers who want to keep it cheap and keep their sanity in the process will adopt this one-step-at-a-time approach to reflective processing in a collaborative structure.

Reflecting Frequently on Process

Regular reflection on the part of students involved in discussions or group work should be part of the process as well. Teachers can brainstorm with students what behaviors and norms need to be part of any paired conversation or collaborative activity. From this initial brainstormed list (which may include good listening skills, supportive body language, avoiding rabbit trails, and establishing and maintaining eye contact) can come a series of questions students might ask themselves after taking part in a structured conversation or collaborative activity:

- Did we get to work quickly?
- Did we avoid getting sidetracked?
- Did we listen supportively and without passing judgment?
- Did we display supportive body language?
- Did we acknowledge each other at the end of the conversation or activity?

Basketball coaches understand that creating a winning team is not just about developing skills (e.g., dribbling, shooting, and passing); it is every bit as much about moving players deliberately and consistently on a continuum from group to team. I believe *students* have a basic understanding of the characteristics of a smooth functioning team; the teacher's job in this case is to surface those understandings and lead students in a discussion of their relative importance. Teachers can tap into what students already know about team building and can, at the same time, add their own insights and develop a set of expectations that allow students to move along that group-to-team continuum week by week and month by month during the school year. Teachers who put students in groups without building in a reflective capacity aimed at continuous improvement are perhaps destined to dislike collaborative work and thus avoid it altogether in favor of individual seat work.

The extent to which paired conversations and more sophisticated and complicated collaborative activities actually work, then, is in direct proportion to the investment of time teachers devote to establishing expectations and improving process. Teachers can and must become relentless in their pursuit of collaboration and teamwork, relying on the reflective capacity of their students, combined with experience, to adjust behavior and develop a skill set that allows for engagement, efficiency, and improving process in the bargain.

Harnessing the VAK Predicates

For those students who are *high auditory* and *high kinesthetic*, everything we have explored so far works well within their learning modes.

Being high auditory does not simply mean that the student enjoys lecture, although that will probably be the case. Auditory learners find enjoyment in talking to others, being read to, and listening to audiotapes (Gregory, 2005, pp. 25–26). I am high auditory, and at any given time I have a couple of taped lectures and books on tape (fiction and nonfiction) in my car. High kinesthetic learners thrive on the movement we have highlighted in this chapter. In a lecture environment, kinesthetic learners are often frustrated and find ways to act out.

I recently observed a student who is undoubtedly high kinesthetic and extremely active (drumming on the floor or desk); he is perfectly content in a classroom that honors four basic ways of processing information: auditory, visual, kinesthetic, and tactile. This same boy drives teachers crazy in classrooms where seatwork and sitting still are the norm. Yet his regular classroom teacher has no problems with him; she understands that students like him need to move, talk, and, yes, *fidget*. I know of teachers who give kids who are highly kinesthetic or tactile a squeeze ball or other object they can manipulate while seated.

Visuals are always an important part of a multidimensional approach to learning. There are those among us who need diagrams, charts, maps, pictures, or graphic organizers in order to provide clarity, organize thoughts, and deepen understanding. Lecture, a much-preferred method of instructional delivery, is mainly auditory. Direct instruction that involves lecture can be enhanced and reinforced by providing visuals for students. One note of caution concerning the display of visuals: When revealing a picture, cartoon, diagram, photograph, or textual information on the screen, *pause long enough to let students read it or process the image or copy.* As you reveal the image on the screen, *do not look at the students.* Turn and look at the image yourself, and stand stock still with your hands at your sides. Their eyes will follow your eyes to the screen, and in the words of Michael Grinder (2000), "since the two parties, namely the teacher and the student, are looking at a third point, the communication is referred to as *three-point* communication" (p. 138). Teachers who look at the kids while revealing something on the screen create dissonance. The student does not know whether to look at the teacher or at the image on the screen. I have tested this more times than I can count with students and adults alike, and in every case, I can create problems by simply making eye contact with them while at the same time expecting them to look at the screen. When I look at the screen, *they look at the screen.*

In observing classrooms over the years, I have seen many cases where teachers will reveal an image and then *continue to talk while the students are trying to come to grips with the image.* When this happens, dissonance is created and students lose focus. Allen (2002) gives teachers a simple yet effective way to prevent the confusion that is likely to result from dueling auditory and visual input. Once an image has been projected or displayed to the students, Alan cautions, "Don't talk for a moment and give students a chance to put all their attention on understanding the visual. It's that easy." Once it is apparent that "everyone has seen and feels comfortable with the new information," the teacher can continue speaking (p. 96).

The same principle applies when teachers reveal a piece of text on the screen and *then proceed to read it to the students.* I used to do this and I was clueless about the problems I created for the students until one of them pointed it out to me on a year-end evaluation instrument I gave my kids in early June. It was a seventh grader who provided me with a blinding glimpse of the obvious. *He could not read and listen to me at the same time, especially since I was ahead of him in the text.* The way to deal with this, of course, is to let the kids read whatever you put on the screen while you read it silently with them. I find that when I do this, I finish a bit before most of them and then I can glance at the kids (or adults) from the side of the room to read the body language that tells me they are done. Then I move back to the front of the room and continue the lesson.

Final Thoughts

Classroom teachers at any grade level would do well, then, to create a classroom culture that supports students who are kinesthetic, visual, tactile, and auditory. Perhaps the philosophical underpinning of differentiation is the understanding that students process information and ultimately learn in different ways. Due to my predilection for all things auditory, early in my teaching career I tended to lecture for the simple reason that I felt comfortable with it. I became a much more effective teacher when I began to realize that not everyone learned the way I did.

When teachers take the time to invest in ways to shift their students from passive observers to active and interdependent learners, the costs associated with the teacher-centered classroom decrease. Getting students actively engaged in their own learning increases their interest (and investment) in the proceedings and, in the long run, keeps it cheap for everyone. As we have seen, however, student engagement comes with a price: proper planning that looks ahead to what might happen and deals with process before trying to deal with content. Teachers who do not take this proactive approach and instead wait on events may face problems in the execution.

For example, a teacher who is considering having students stand, move across the classroom, and find a partner with whom a discussion will take place needs to think ahead as to what might happen. A student could refuse to meet with so-and-so. Students not familiar with the topic for discussion may not be able to take part in a paired conversation. Others might express impatience or ambivalence with a partner, something that may derail the whole conversation. Teachers who take the time to think about all these possibilities can plan ahead and have students talk about something with which they are totally familiar before moving on to content about which they feel less confident. This frontloading of time and effort prior to lesson delivery will pay dividends immediately and is all part of being proactive rather than reactive.

Finally, unless teachers are willing to work with students on improving process when involving them in paired or group activities, progress will not be made and an entire lesson may collapse—at which point everyone loses. After several abortive (and noisy) attempts at engaging students collaboratively, teachers may simply throw in the towel and return to more traditional seat work—less effective when it comes to learning but more effective when it comes to maintaining a quiet classroom.

Chapter 5 provides an opportunity to deal with the issue of feedback in the continuous improvement cycle. As every coach knows, feedback is a critical part of that cycle. As we'll see, providing it is powerful and *not* providing it can get expensive in many ways. We'll also discover that feedback can come in many forms and from many sources, not just the teacher.

5

Harnessing the Power of Feedback

Mr. Halladay, a fourth-grade teacher, has become a master at giving what Susan Brookhart (2008) calls "quick and quiet" feedback. While his students are involved in seatwork, Mr. Halladay moves from desk to desk in what he describes as a "hunkering down" position. Crouching next to Sheila's desk, he gives her one or two specific pieces of feedback that will help improve her next essay. Handing her the essay, on which the feedback is recorded, he compliments her on her use of verb-subject agreement, a recent area of improvement for Sheila. Finally, he asks if she has any questions, thanks her, and moves on to yet another student. With this kind of individual feedback, as Brookhart notes, it is not necessary "to broadcast to the class which particular difficulty one student is having" (p. 49). Mr. Halladay also understands that even praise may best be delivered privately, especially if some students have an aversion to being praised publicly. These quick and quiet visits by Mr. Halladay occur whenever students are involved in seat work and they leave students with meaningful feedback that they appreciate and have come to realize is an important part of their continuous improvement process.

It is a sad fact that in our often headlong rush to cover the material in many subject areas, feedback becomes a casualty. According to Konold, Miller, and Konold (2004), "Unfortunately, it is easy to become engrossed in lesson content and many other teaching-related responsibilities and subsequently forget about the importance and benefits of providing high-quality feedback" (p. 64). After delving into the research surrounding the nature, uses, and level of use of feedback, Hattie and Temperley (2007) conclude, in the *Review of Educational Research,* that "it is difficult to document the frequency of feedback in classrooms, except to note that it is low" (p. 100). Feedback, once understood, should be part of every teacher's instructional program.

Providing feedback begins with an examination of student work and with an understanding of students' strengths and weaknesses on the part of the teacher. In a meta-analysis of the research on classroom assessment, Black and William (1998) speak of the flexibility teachers need in order to serve their students along the continuous improvement highway.

> We start from the self-evident proposition that teaching and learning must be interactive. Teachers need to know about their pupils' progress and difficulties with learning so that they can adapt their own work to meet pupils' needs—needs that are often unpredictable and that can vary from one pupil to another. Teachers can find out what they need to know in a variety of ways, including observation and discussion in the classroom and the reading of pupils' work. (p. 140)

Simply having identified what students need to do to improve is of little value unless it is communicated to them, and that communication needs to be specific and, above all, *of some actual use to the students.*

Marzano, Pickering, and Pollock (2001), after examining several studies on the effect of providing feedback, conclude that "simply telling students that their answer on a test is right or wrong has a negative effect on achievement. [Moreover, the] best feedback appears to involve an explanation as to what is accurate and what is inaccurate in terms of student responses" (p. 96). So check marks and letter grades may give teachers something for their grade books, but they provide little to help students improve. Kaufeldt (2005) affirms that as students are engaged in completing projects and assignments, "avoid grading the tasks that students do and instead give accurate feedback—formally and informally—checking for progress at designated benchmarks" (p. 144). Kaufeldt adds that when students know a grade is on the immediate horizon, "the risk is greater and they are likely to feel more anxiety about the resulting product" (p. 144).

Feinstein (2004) relates the following feedback regarding how the brain learns:

> Feedback is required to clarify and correct the information we receive; it allows the brain to readjust and reevaluate what it thinks it knows. Feedback is best when it is corrective in nature, explaining what students did right and wrong. Positive feedback—which can include suggestions about how to improve or change—helps us cope with stress. (p. 39)

We need to get kids to understand that feedback is *all* positive if it does what it is intended to do, which is to allow kids to make course corrections as necessary. We need to explain (and demonstrate) to students that feedback is not personal and is not intended as negative criticism. Feedback is simply a normal and necessary part of the continuous improvement journey for all of us.

Letter or number grades as a form of feedback are comparative rather than descriptive in nature, according to Popham (2008), and do not tell students much except where they rank in relation to others in the class. Grades provide little traction because they don't, by themselves, provide the kind of specific information that allows a student to make adjustments in performance. Descriptive feedback, according to Popham (2008), "indicates what students can currently do in order to achieve a target curricular aim or master an en route building block related to that aim" (p. 114). Seeing a "Well done!" in red ink on an essay does not provide a student with any real information. Knowing that 20% of his answers on a test are incorrect again says little. As useful feedback mechanisms, grades come up short because, in the words of Alfie Kohn (1999), "they don't provide accurate and reliable information about how students are doing" (p. 41).

My experience has been that feedback is not welcomed by kids (or adults!) when it ceases to be objective and is perceived as judgmental. Costa (2008) describes *nonjudgmental* feedback as "a process whereby concrete and specific factual information about a group's thinking, decisions, and actions are provided so that the group can use the information for self-validation, self-correction, or self-modification" (p. 150). The same can be said of individuals, who will respond better to feedback that is clear, specific, and factual.

Suggested Feedback Mechanisms

At this point, we shift our attention from why meaningful feedback is a critical component of the learning process to ways of providing that feedback—something that will continue into the next chapter in a formal discussion of formative and summative feedback. Specifically, what can teachers do to satisfy the students' needs to have their good work and progress acknowledged, while at the same time providing the corrective feedback that will help kids meet their goals and successfully complete the assigned tasks?

Checklists and Rubrics as Signposts

Mr. Halladay made a point of giving frequent, meaningful feedback on a one-to-one basis, taking the time to stop and hunker down next to a student, providing praise and suggestions for a change of direction in that student's continuous improvement journey. Two other feedback tools are checklists and rubrics, which are intended to help students self-evaluate and self-adjust while working on a specific task. A checklist might be as simple as the "process for completing a complicated task like writing a narrative essay," according to Burke (2006, p. 103). While students may still need a teacher's help along the way to completing a task, a checklist serves as a road map that allows them to move down the road with far less outside assistance.

Another effective form of ongoing and concrete feedback for students is the rubric. The same rubric that provides teachers with the criteria for grading can provide students with guidelines for their work. In this way the teacher and the student are on, literally, the same page when working toward the completion of a project or task. During most of my teaching career, I knew little about rubrics. When I graded projects or essays, I knew what I was looking for, but students often had no idea. It was not until a couple of decades into my career that I began using some simple and effective rubrics, including one for student oral presentations.

Rubrics allow students to self-assess and, according to Burke (2006), "answer their own question of 'How good is good enough?'" (p. 130). Checklists can be turned into rubrics and rubrics can be tied to content standards, says Burke (2006), adding that rubrics are helpful "because they describe what the student needs to do to move from a score of '2' to a score of '3' in order to improve to meet the standard" (p. 135). Students who are able to answer their own basic questions as they relate to process and quality are less likely to need the intervention of teachers on this continuous improvement highway.

Two Examples of Rubrics

The rubric in Figure 5.1 is a simple four-point rubric. It tells students exactly what is needed to receive a four, the rubric's highest rating, when including quotations in support of research done as part of a term paper.

Figure 5.1 Rubric for a Quotation

Quotation	①	②	③	④
Student includes an appropriate quotation to support research	• includes a quotation • cites author	• cites title of author (president of FDA, scientist, board member)	• cites the source (*Newsweek*) • cites the date	• supports the arguments • is punctuated correctly

From Burke, K. (2006). *From Standards to Rubrics in 6 Steps: Tools for Assessing Student Learning, K–8.* Thousand Oaks, CA: Corwin.

Having a well-constructed rubric at his or her fingertips allows a student to self-evaluate in terms of the *quality* of a given task or project. Specifically, as stated by Burke (2006), rubrics are really scoring guides "designed to provide constructive feedback to students by helping them think more clearly about the characteristics of quality work" (p. 126). Depka (2006) supplies the three basic steps in creating a rubric:

1. Choose a point scale.

2. Identify criteria that will lead to the successful completion of the product, project, or performance to be evaluated.

3. Write descriptors of quality for each criterion at each point value. (p. 55)

Depka provides an example of a holistic rubric (one that contains several descriptors for each of the point values) in Figure 5.2.

Looking at all this from the standpoint of the teacher, whose enemy is time and who wants to be able to find quality time at home after hours, *every bit of incremental classroom feedback provided as a matter of course will save tons of time after school and on weekends.* Checklists and rubrics, to a great extent, take teachers out of the equation and assist students in developing more self-reliance and responsibility. For the students, it provides reassurance and clarification; these are two ingredients necessary to reduce stress and improve performance. Checklists and rubrics together comprise a very cost-conscious approach to the continuous improvement process.

Figure 5.2   PowerPoint Presentation Rubric: Mrs. Smith's Fourth-Grade Class

4 Points	• Title has accurate spelling and capitalization, relates to the project, and catches audience interest. • Eight slides include at least four related pictures and two related graphs or charts. Color, sound, and transitions enhance presentation. • Each slide contains accurate, easy-to-understand, in-depth information to support the topic.
3 Points	• Title has accurate spelling and capitalization and relates to the project. • Eight slides include at least four related pictures and two related graphs or charts. • Each slide contains accurate, easy-to-understand information to support the topic.
2 Points	• Title has accurate spelling and capitalization. • Eight slides include at least four related pictures. • Each slide contains accurate, easy-to-understand information to support the topic.
1 Point	• Title is present. • Eight slides are present. • Information in each slide supports the topic.

From Depka, E. (2006). *The Data Guidebook for Teachers and Leaders: Tools for Continuous Improvement.* Thousand Oaks, CA: Corwin.

Instruction Meets Assessment

Another method for checking student progress is the portfolio, which is, according to Burke (2005), not "just a collection of stuff randomly organized and stuck in a folder" (p. 56). A useful and effective portfolio is, as defined by Carr and Harris (2001), a "purposeful, integrated collection of student work showing effort, progress, or achievement in one or more areas" (cited in Burke, 2005, p. 56). Portfolios, in order to avoid being the aforementioned "collection of stuff," need to be carefully and purposefully planned and executed. What goes into the students' portfolios may be a combination of items chosen by teachers, students, or even parents, but it needs to provide "evidence that the students met school goals or standards and that they understand the basic concepts of the course" (Burke, 2005, p. 61).

In terms of portfolio items, collecting and keeping track of—and not losing—everything that needs to be part of the final product has become a less cumbersome and onerous task in the twenty-first century. Computer software programs have made it "far easier for students to gather a diverse set of materials and share them across geographies and technical platforms" (Regan, 2008, p. 5). Combining a purposeful, standards-connected (if that is required) portfolio assessment program with twenty-first-century technology gives teachers a powerful tool to check student progress. It also gives teachers the opportunity to give feedback to students along the way.

The combination of timely feedback and clear evidence of steady progress is, in my experience, a powerful motivator for students. Portfolios provide an opportunity for students to set their own achievement goals and see the progress reflected in the output during the various stages of improvement. Progress is difficult to measure, however, if students and teachers don't have some idea as to what the eventual goal is, whether it is determined by a school or state standard or chosen by students and teachers working in tandem on the continuous improvement process.

Goal Setting and Gap Elimination

Goals are critical elements in this progress because they give students a clear understanding of where they want to go relative to where they are now. Stretching into the distance between where Eddie is now and where Eddie and his teacher have agreed he should be (the goal) is a gap that can only be closed if Eddie wants to close it. My experience is that if students can see tangible progress along a predetermined path, their motivation level is high. If there is no goal and if all Eddie receives is a letter grade or "atta boy" on his most recent essay, the lack of information and feedback tells him little and provides even less in the way of internal motivation.

Having studied the research relating to the effectiveness of goal setting on student achievement, Marzano (2003b) affirms that there is a significant and positive relationship between the two. Marzano also suggests that "establishing goals for individual students is perhaps more powerful than setting a few schoolwide goals" (p. 46). Many of us have been part of teams or committees that have set such building-level goals only to have the process grind to a halt with the articulation of several admirable expectations and their inclusion in a binder. Admirable though the goals may be, they may in fact never translate into application at the classroom level. Success in classrooms is a bottom-up procedure whereby the attainment of an individual goal on Eddie's part moves the class one step closer to the achievement of classroom or school-wide goals. Absent action at the classroom level, however, goals arrived at by teams within the school will remain unfulfilled.

On the road to improvement, Marzano (2003b) says that "challenging goals must be set for all students; second, effective feedback must be specific and formative" (p. 46). He also recommends that schools begin to use "innovative report cards that use formative classroom assessments" (p. 46). The checklists, rubrics, and portfolios we explored earlier in this chapter would provide a parent who wants to see how her son or daughter is progressing with much needed and much appreciated feedback.

Importance of Feedback Specificity

When a teacher is checking grammar in a piece of writing, the job of providing feedback is fairly simple. A comma or period belongs there or it does not. The sentence is complete or it is a fragment. Marking through what is incorrect with a red pen does not give students enough information to make corrections or understand what is wrong. Konold, Miller, and Konold (2004) put it this way: "Written feedback should include positive remarks about the student's work and provide corrective feedback in a prominent manner. . . . Specific comments are more beneficial than simply circling or underlining the student's errors" (p. 68).

Earlier in this chapter we cautioned against the use of judgmental feedback. Every day in every school in America teachers use words like *good*, *right*, and *wrong* in automatic reactions to student statements or answers. These words are loaded, according to Brooks and Brooks (1999). "Upon hearing these words, students either continue or alter their thinking, not because of some internal realization but because of an external prompt. Over time, this sort of feedback makes students teacher-dependent" (p. 94). Students who may already be fairly certain that education is all about right and wrong answers may simply shut down and not risk answers, statements, or opinions they think stand a fairly good chance of being incorrect.

This is not to say, however, that teachers should not indicate when a student is wrong. Konold, Miller, and Konold (2004) differentiate between incorrect student responses that are simply careless mistakes and those that can be attributed to a lack of knowledge or understanding of the subject. In the case of the former, the teacher "can simply provide the correct answer and continue on with the lesson."

In the latter case, however, "prompts or cues that lead the student to the correct response are appropriate" (p. 65). Virginia's 1999 Teacher of the Year and former elementary teacher, Linda Koutoufas (2007), said she "eventually created a class of risk-takers—students who were not afraid to risk unique and brilliant answers because they knew they would be supported and that, if incorrect, I would take the time to guide them to a correct answer" (p. 117). Teachers like Koutoufas, who take the time to guide students gently and relentlessly toward success one small step at a time, remind us that teaching is not about the answers. It is about the kids, and it is about making early investments that can lead to huge payoffs in the end. Investing early helps keep costs low later on.

The Thing About Praise

Teachers who respond with automatic praise to every bit of input from students are not being helpful because such phrases as "Good work!" or "Great job!" or "Well done!" don't really provide students with much useful information. Writing on instruction at the college level, Ehrlich and Zoltek (2006) caution that "instructors who praise every answer are put in an awkward position when confronted with incorrect or vague responses" (p. 9). When students are brave enough to offer opinions, ask questions, or provide answers in class, teachers need to take the time to think about how to respond and then respond appropriately—providing acknowledgement of what is correct and offering corrective feedback when necessary. Feedback must help the student make midcourse adjustments and corrections.

Praise can be overused and it may have unintended and negative consequences—especially if the praise is public. "Student response to teacher praise can be expected to vary from highly positive through neutral to highly negative," according to Brophy (1981), who goes on to point out that a student who may be "fighting a 'teacher's pet' image" with his peers is "less likely to repeat the behavior that was praised" (p. 20). Teachers need to consider this, observe carefully what the effect of verbal praise is on students, and act accordingly.

I once worked for a supervisor who, on her first day on the job as our director, sent each of us in the office an e-mail asking how we wanted to be praised, publicly or privately. She then followed through and did exactly what we requested. Those of us who preferred to be praised privately were never praised publicly. Having students put their preference concerning praise on an index card at the beginning of the year would make things far less expensive down the road. This is yet another case of investing up front in order to avoid expensive mistakes later on.

Instructive Feedback

Teachers can enhance feedback beyond a simple "That is correct, Tony!" by utilizing what Werts, Wolery, Gast, and Holcombe (1996) call instructive feedback, which involves "presenting extra information in the consequent (feedback) events following students' responses during direct instruction" (p. 70). For example, suppose a social studies teacher asks students to identify one of the key functions of the president of the United States and gets the answer "commander in chief" from Carol. "That is correct, Carol," might be followed by delving into the other functions connected to the office of president. According to Werts et al., "When brief verbal or visual instructive feedback is used, session length does not increase—but the amount of learning does" (p. 71).

Teachers Need Feedback Too

In addition to providing direct feedback for students, teachers can facilitate their own feedback opportunities. When I was a middle school teacher, I sometimes had myself videotaped while teaching. Looking at these tapes provided me with much laughter and many opportunities to bury my face in my hands and mumble something to the effect of, "Is that really me?" (It really was.) Looking at those tapes (and listening to them with the picture off so I could concentrate on verbals) gave me much valuable information about my skills as a teacher. I found, for example, that my hands and arms were sometimes all over the place. I looked more like a cheerleader than a teacher. My out-of-control gestures must have been terribly distracting for my students, and I was able to adjust those movements based on what I observed in the tapes. By listening with the picture off, I found that I tended to speak so quickly that I could not keep up with the flow. If it affected me in this way, how must it have affected my students? That meant I had to concentrate on speaking more slowly. Without the tapes (and the feedback they gave me) I would have continued in those unfortunate habits.

Matthew Dicks, a third-grade teacher in Connecticut, regularly tapes himself and his students using a digital camera. Says Dicks (2005), "By turning the camera on ourselves, we receive immediate feedback on teaching and learning behaviors in the classroom" (p. 78).

Students tape their own experiments in science "and use the footage to report and assess their work" (p. 79). He tapes book talks and peer conferences, and his students, steeped in the culture of video games and the internet, receive the immediate feedback they have come to expect. In this way, Dicks serves as a facilitator of visual and auditory feedback that he and his third graders value.

A good friend of mine suggests that teachers keep a journal in which they describe on a daily or weekly basis what works and does not work in the classroom. A whole section of the journal could be devoted to feedback tools and the extent to which each is successful—and under what circumstances. This kind of journaling can remind teachers about details they may not remember, but which may be important. For example, if public praise does not work for two or three kids in the class, a journal entry can capture that fact so that, going forward, praise given to those students can be given privately.

I suggest that teachers invite their colleagues to observe in their classrooms on a regular basis. My experience is that observations like this are most effective when the observer knows exactly what to look for, as requested by the classroom teacher. For example, a teacher being observed might like to know if her hand and arm gestures are distracting, or if she is allowing some think time after asking a question of the class. In the appendix, I will provide a whole list of *look fors* that might help an observer provide valuable feedback to the classroom teacher—feedback that can allow the teacher to make necessary adjustments and changes that will, in the future, help keep it cheap!

When I taught seventh grade, I spent the last day of school having students evaluate me in several areas. That document gave me much valuable information. However, there was one problem: The data I received on the evaluations did not help those particular students. It certainly assisted me in the *following* school year, but for them it was a dollar short and several months too late. Had I sought feedback from them every nine weeks, for example, I could have used it to improve my performance as a teacher all year long.

In seeking student input, there is no need to create a long or elaborate teacher-evaluation instrument for use in the classroom. A simple Plus-Delta chart (Figure 5.3) invites students to comment on what the teacher is doing effectively (the Plus column) and on what he or she could do to improve (the Delta column). Even better than collecting the data would be discussing with the students the comments they wrote on the Delta side and indicating which

Figure 5.3   Plus-Delta Chart

Student-to-Teacher Feedback	
+	**Δ**

changes will be instituted because of their feedback. Then, of course, the changes must be implemented or the integrity of the exercise will be lost.

Students can provide other students with valuable feedback during paired or group conversations, or by reading each other's essay or report drafts. When I was a junior high school yearbook adviser, stories for the yearbook had to be read by at least three yearbook staff members. By the time the drafts got to me, there was a great deal of written feedback on the drafts. I added my two cents and gave it back to the staff member who had written the story for a final rewrite. While students cannot, of course, assign grades, they can certainly provide another set of eyes and another perspective along the way for a project, essay, article, or speech.

Feedback, then, can come from many sources. Teachers, peers, and rubrics can provide the information students need in order to make midcourse corrections that will take them to their ultimate destination—the successful completion of a given task or assignment. Once again, students need to understand that it is perfectly normal to make mistakes and that *feedback is simply a way to discover those mistakes, make adjustments, and move on to the successful completion of a project or task.*

Stress the Positive

Brookhart (2007/2008) suggests teachers avail themselves of every opportunity to "give students positive messages about how they are doing relative to the learning targets and what might be useful to do next" (p. 59). The messages can be verbal or written and should be clear enough to help students adjust their thinking and improve their work.

> Unsuccessful learners have sometimes been so frustrated by their school experiences that they might see every attempt to help them as just another declaration that they are "stupid." For these learners, point out improvements over their previous performance, even if those improvements don't amount to overall success on the assignment. Then select one or two small, doable next steps. After the next round of work, give the student feedback on his or her success with those steps, and so on. (Brookhart, 2007/2008, pp. 56–57)

Mr. Halladay, the fictitious fourth-grade teacher at the beginning of this chapter, made certain that he found something related to improvement, no matter how minor, before he hunkered down at a particular student's desk. He ended his quick and quiet visit with that positive message.

Investing in Collaborative Feedback Research

Conversations with colleagues about their feedback techniques might well assist individual teachers in adding to their own repertoire of effective feedback strategies. Administrators can provide time at faculty meetings to have teachers discuss feedback, look at the research, and come to some conclusions about how everyone can handle feedback in the building. A brainstorming session where feedback techniques are charted and discussed might serve as the foundation for a feedback booklet that can be distributed to teachers in the building.

Book talks built around the works of authors who have done a good deal of research and reporting on effective feedback techniques would benefit teachers and students alike. Administrators who take part in these sessions would benefit as well when it comes time to provide their own formative feedback to teachers after classroom observations. In addition, teachers can certainly check with other teachers in their school or district to see what kind of feedback has been most useful and successful. Collaborating with others can yield not only feedback strategies, but other examples of effective instruction, relationship building, and process management.

An Early Lesson in Feedback

I began coauthoring my first book, *The Underground Cave,* when I was eleven; my friend Gary and I finished it the next year. We came up with a cast of characters, setting and plot, a few soft lead pencils, and a lined tablet I still possess. With that, we began our great adventure. He would write a few pages, I would write a few pages, and as we wrote, two of our teachers provided practical and valuable feedback. They provided encouragement, my aunt supplied a typewriter (electric!), I hunted-and-pecked my way through countless mimeograph masters, and we came up with a bestselling mystery. We sold fifty copies. I think my grandmother bought half of them. We had our pictures taken and a feature story in the local newspaper highlighted our success. We went on to write *The Mystery at Broken Canoe,* in honor of our brand new state, Alaska (which shows my age). By the time we were teenagers, our fledgling writing careers waned as we became interested in sports and other things.

While we wrote, we learned from our teachers that the period goes inside the quotation marks. Our teachers assisted us in making adjustments concerning subject-verb agreement. We made a careful study of the use of dialogue as modeled in the Hardy Boys and Nancy Drew mystery stories. We made mistakes and adjustments, and it took several months to complete our magnum opus. Without the support of those teachers, I doubt we would have finished one, let alone two, books. Remembering the experience of authoring those two thin mimeographed volumes still makes me smile, and I share this joy in my workshops. *Success tastes good.*

Education should be one long, continuous-improvement feast. For kids who have tasted the satisfaction that comes from doing something today that they could not do yesterday, it is just that. To me, that is what education is all about. Gary and I did not care if we made any money, and at a retail price of fifteen cents per copy, profit was not a motive. Our motivation came from within. Our reward was intrinsic. We got no stickers for completing it. We received no grade. The *true value* of doing something difficult *is in the doing*—and we enjoyed what we did. But we could not have done it without support from our teachers and from each other. It was a team effort all around.

We also had a clear notion of what we wanted to accomplish. Throughout the long process, we received feedback from each other and from our teachers, and we kept our eyes on the goal. Along the way, we picked up countless grammatical principles and our writing improved. There were no quizzes, no tests, and no worksheets in our journey. We dreamed and we wrote. It was the ultimate performance task, and we did it for the very best of reasons: because we wanted to.

Without a goal, even the best feedback will likely not succeed. The goal comes first, followed by the steps inherent in its attainment. Feedback "needs to describe where the student is in relation to the learning goal" (Brookhart, 2008, p. 56). Thinking back to our childhood coauthorship of *The Underground Cave,* Gary and I always had a destination in mind. We were clear about what we wanted and about where we wanted to go. This clarity, along with external feedback provided by teachers, peers, and relatives, accelerated our progress toward the book's completion and publication. We were self-motivated and self-published. We just needed a little help from our friends.

Final Thoughts

Feedback is inseparably connected to quality instruction. The efficacy of the feedback is dependent on the efficacy of the instruction in any classroom. Feedback, according to Hattie and Temperley (2007), "can only build on something; it is of little use when there is no initial learning or surface information" (p. 104). The two go hand in hand. Instruction without feedback makes for lackluster performance on the part of students who have no earthly idea where they are in the continuous improvement journey. The foundation of a good rubric or any good feedback tool is good instruction. When a student knows he will receive feedback that is corrective, descriptive, and ultimately useful, he just may become more interested in the outcome.

In Chapter 6, we'll expand our discussion of feedback with a look at the whole issue of formative versus summative assessment. Specifically, we'll look at which of those two forms of assessment is more cost-effective in terms of student achievement and student success.

6

Balancing Formative and Summative Assessment

Mr. Renfro, a first-year seventh-grade middle school social studies teacher, was a believer in combining content with process. One of his own high school history teachers was known for having her students write essays frequently, and she did not just check for accuracy in terms of content: she was a stickler for the mechanics of grammar, writing style . . . the whole nine yards. Mr. Renfro's college career was made far easier by this teacher who challenged her students in every way and took no prisoners. Mr. Renfro decided that he would offer his students this same level of rigor and assigned weekly essays to all four of his seventh-grade classes.

He did not grade these essays, but he made it his habit to provide plenty of written feedback prior to handing them back to students. Time was provided in class for students to start their work on that week's essay, and he required that they continue their work at home before handing the assignment in on Friday. After a month or so, Mr. Renfro noticed two things: First, students had a lot of questions during the week related to the mechanics of writing an essay, and while students worked in class he spent a good deal of his time running from desk to desk in order to assist his students. Second, he spent much of his weekend providing the kind of meaningful and specific feedback he knew would serve his students well now and in the future.

A veteran eighth-grade English teacher in his building applauded Mr. Renfro's efforts at improving his students' writing skills and suggested that he use a writing rubric that she used in her classes on a regular basis. She explained its use to Mr. Renfro and even offered to come into one of his classes during her preparation period to explain it to his students. Mr. Renfro took her up on her offer, and when the next batch of essays was completed and handed in he again noticed two things: First, the number of student questions related to writing mechanics decreased significantly over the last prerubric batch. Second, he spent a good deal less time on weekends checking the papers.

What Mr. Renfro discovered, thanks to some advice and assistance from the eighth-grade English teacher in his building, was that using a simple writing rubric made it possible for students to check their own progress in a very concrete way. As his students' understanding of and facility with the rubric improved, so did their essays. Mr. Renfro shifted a great deal of the workload from himself to them and in the process helped to make them independent learners. Absent in this case was the pressure of a grade; feedback for the students was immediate, and checking for understanding in terms of the mechanics of writing was frequent. Marzano (2006) affirms that "formative classroom assessment can and should begin immediately within a learning episode and span its entire duration" (p. 9).

Good coaches are experts at giving good and frequent feedback. In the words of Fisher and Frey (2007), "coaching involves repeated cycles of ongoing assessment, feedback, and instruction as the primary means for improving individual and team performance." Moreover, according to Fisher and Frey, "success in the 'game,' in this case, the summative assessment, begins in practice" (p. vii). Combine sufficient conditioning with plenty of feedback in practice, along with opportunities to fold that feedback into the practice sessions, and other things being equal, the team should do well on Friday night or Saturday afternoon. This cycle is one of continuous improvement, and it applies to the classroom every bit as much as to the swimming pool or the gymnasium.

Tomlinson and McTighe (2006) recommend that "teachers should build into their instructional plans regular opportunities for feedback and refinement" (p. 79). "All types of learning," according to Tomlinson and McTighe, "whether on the practice field or in the classroom, require feedback" (p. 77). Unless players or students know what they have done that needs to be corrected, and are affirmed in those things they are already doing correctly, it is difficult to see how they could improve.

All of which brings us to a larger discussion concerning the role of assessment in the whole continuous improvement process. What is the difference between formative and summative assessment? When should teachers use the former and when the latter? Which is most helpful to students in terms of their academic development? What are some popular and effective examples of formative assessment? How does feedback fit into the picture in terms of both summative and formative assessment? Will using formative assessment allow teachers to avoid the expense associated with poor performance on summative tests?

Summative and Formative Assessment

Popham (2008) provides us with a short, clear definition of these two forms of assessment: "Formative assessment is a way to improve the caliber of still-underway instructional activities and summative assessment [is] a way to determine the effectiveness of already-completed instructional activities" (p. 4). Summative assessments come in the form of graded quizzes or tests at the end of a unit, grading period, or course. Such assessments provide grades, of course, but in terms of feedback for students, such grades are of little use since the game is over for that unit or that material. The tendency on the part of teachers is to record the grades and, perhaps, lament that the results were not better.

Summative test results *can* provide feedback for teachers. On those occasions when I conducted an item analysis and discovered that sixty-five percent of the kids in my class missed questions twenty-five through twenty-eight (all of which were related to one topic or concept), that told me something related to my instruction. It told me that I did a less-than-stellar job of covering that particular topic and I needed to correct that for the next year. Unfortunately, it still meant that my students had a poor grasp of the material related to those four test questions. I made a note to adjust my teaching in the coming year and then moved on in my curriculum.

State assessments are also summative, and those results can be used from year to year to improve student performance by indicating areas where instruction may be weak. The results of a state writing assessment may indicate that a teacher needs to spend more time with next year's students stressing particular writing skills. As with summative assessments in the classroom, item analyses may indicate a weakness in the test itself, and adjustments may have to be made.

Once again, as with classroom tests at the end of a chapter, unit, or grading period, the emphasis in terms of improvement is on *next* year and is of little help to this set of students.

Limits of Summative Testing

Armstrong (2006) points out that these ubiquitous standardized tests, far from being valuable learning experiences, are in fact "*interruptions* in the actual experiences of learning" (p. 40). Adds Burke (2005), "Testing has always been separate from learning" (p. xx). Moreover, "emphasis has been placed on the summative or end evaluation where it is discovered what the student does and doesn't know—often too late to do anything about it" (Burke, p. xx).

It is not just the tests themselves that interrupt the learning process, but *test preparation* seems to have become a national obsession. In the weeks leading up to end-of-year testing, teachers may spend a great deal of time reviewing and otherwise preparing students for the tests. My experience is that this discourages the kind of in-depth learning we need to encourage and replaces it with a headlong rush to cover the material. I recently heard of a high school senior, a top student in his class, who said that he spent so much time studying for tests that *he did not have time to learn.*

That high-achieving student will succeed in spite of the testing culture that seems to prevail in education today. On the other hand, overreliance on summative assessments that do not provide useful feedback to students can lead to what Black and William (1998) call a "cycle of repeated failure" where students "who get low marks this time also got low marks last time and come to expect to get low marks next time" (p. 144). These students lack self-confidence, at least in part because the speed with which material is covered does not allow for the kind of constructive and useful feedback that could break that cycle of failure.

In a testing-obsessed age, teachers need to understand clearly the nature and uses of summative assessment, as well as what it does not accomplish for Eddie and his classmates. If we provide Eddie with feedback and new opportunities for him to use the feedback so that he can improve his performance in key areas, *the summative tests will take care of themselves.* Kids who taste success day after day will build confidence, and that confidence will carry over into any summative exercise that the teacher, the school district, or the state can send their way.

The Cost of Cramming

One final problem with summative quizzes and tests should provide teachers with a very good reason to limit their use in the classroom. Kids, left to their own devices, take part in the time-honored ritual of cramming. The object, if Eddie understands it correctly, is to get a high score on the quiz. He is, through long experience, pretty certain that those ten items will not see the light of day after this particular quiz, so actually learning the material by committing it to long-term memory may not be necessary. It is enough to pass the quiz, something that requires only a little strategic, last-minute cramming the evening before, or even on the bus on the way to school.

Sprenger (2005) references research by Crew (1969) that indicates "that students who crammed for the test the day before for two hours scored considerably higher than those who did not," but significantly, Crew also found that "students who crammed did not retain the knowledge" (p. 130). So the short-term cost to Eddie is low—a few minutes to cram for a quiz or an hour or so to do the same for a test—and score as high as possible on the assessment. If getting a good grade is the goal, Eddie may be in good shape, but if *actually learning the material* is what will serve Eddie best, then his long-term return on the investment from cramming is also low.

In spite of the fact that teachers know very well that students wait until the last minute to load their short-term memory with enough information to get through the quiz or test, the cycle continues apace. Students cram, the grade goes into the book, the quizzes go into the waste basket, and the kids and the teachers move on to repeat this scenario time and again throughout the course of the school year. Jenkins (2005) says that "any educational institution that encourages cramming is unintentionally giving students permission to forget" (p. 1). Eddie has been given permission to forget, then, and the long-term cost to him is very high because, as we stated above, while he has mastered the art of getting by through cramming, *he will not retain the information in long-term memory.*

Summative assessments, then, have their limitations. Quiz and test scores that may or may not be the result of cramming sessions generate a grade. Unfortunately, that grade does not provide the student with any feedback useful for future learning, and the grade itself may not serve as a motivator for students. Deci (1996) conducted an experiment that focused on this whole issue of grades as motivators for students.

We had two groups of college students spend about three hours learning some complex material on neurophysiology—on the machinery of the brain. Half of these students were told they would be tested and graded on their learning, and the others were told they would have the opportunity to put the material to active use by teaching it to others. (p. 47)

After administering a questionnaire that assessed their intrinsic motivation, Deci "found, as expected, that those who learned in order to be tested were less intrinsically motivated" (p. 47). In addition, Deci tested *both* groups on the material, not just the ones whose stated purpose was to prepare for an assessment, "and the results showed that the students who learned in order to enable them to teach others displayed considerably greater conceptual understanding of the material than did the students who learned in order to be tested" (p. 47). This, even though one group of students *had no idea they would be tested while the other fully expected it.*

Advantages of Formative Assessment

All of which brings us back to the whole purpose of assessment, which is to help make Eddie aware of what he does and does not know and subsequently provide him with opportunities to accelerate improvement using feedback. Popham (2008) affirms that "teachers should build and use assessments to gather evidence of what it is that students know and can do, not to compare students' performances with one another" (p. 88). Moreover, Popham continues, "if certain tests are required for grade-giving purposes, as they are in many settings, students' scores on these tests should not be part of the formative assessment process, and teachers should inform students of this fact well in advance" (p. 89). There is no reason students cannot be made aware of the relative uses of these two types of assessment.

Building Quality Control Into the System

We have seen that summative assessments are meant to tell students how they *did* and formative assessments are intended to tell students how they are *doing.* Looking at *how students are doing* along their journey, rather than simply recording *how they have done* at intervals, is a way of building quality control into the system. An advocate for the use of rubrics in English classrooms, Jenkins (2003) points out that "we cannot inspect quality into any process; we must build in the quality" (p. 59). According to Jenkins, "spending Saturday after Saturday after Saturday scoring papers is essentially an attempt to inspect quality into student writing" (p. 59). He concludes that this does not work, and I might add that it is expensive for two reasons: (1) The teacher is doing the work, and (2) if the teacher simply supplies a letter grade or numerical score, it becomes expensive for Eddie, who may simply look at the grade, shrug, put the paper into his textbook or book bag, and move on to something else. Moreover, a low score without any written feedback letting Eddie know exactly what can be done to set things right actually becomes a de-motivator.

Add together frequent checks for understanding, gobs of useful feedback from many sources, chances for students to process information in a nonthreatening way, plus opportunities to apply what has been learned; then *subtract* from that the stress that goes with a letter or numerical grade, and the result should be steady progress and the sort of intrinsic motivation that is tied directly to perceived success. And that brings us to what I have just described—formative assessment—and another opportunity to keep it cheap and get more bang for the buck in the process.

Putting the Horse Before the Cart

Summative versus formative is not an either-or proposition at this point in time. As we have seen, because grades are the norm and because our educational system and our state and national governments rely on standardized testing to gauge improvement, the summative side of assessment is likely to be with us for some time to come. *It is a matter of putting the formative horse before the summative cart.* Students who receive specific, meaningful feedback on their continuous improvement journey through the frequent use of formative assessment should do well as a matter of course on *whatever* summative tests they encounter.

As students move through course content, continually process new information, and wrestle with meaning and new understandings (and misunderstandings), teachers need to take the time to see *where students are* in their academic development. When I first started teaching, I thought this meant asking, "Does anyone have questions?" at the end of a thirty-minute lecture. If they all smiled and said nothing, I assumed I had done a marvelous job and that it was time to move on to new information. I hate to admit that it never occurred to me *that they might not be telling me the whole truth and nothing but the truth.* It wasn't that they intentionally lied; they simply did not understand enough about what we had covered to formulate questions. Also, as a practical matter, students often do not want to admit they do not understand, and raising questions, from their perspective, signals this lack of understanding to their peers.

I know now what I did not understand then: at the point where I asked for questions, they had just spent several minutes sitting, listening to me talk, and taking their own notes. They were still in passive mode, and I was asking them to analyze and synthesize in the length of time it took me to ask, "Does anyone have questions?" I looked expectantly at them even as they looked blankly at me. Kids (and adults, for that matter) *need some time to process the information in some way and, by so doing, to develop some understanding of the new information that was just covered.*

Pausing to Chew on the Information

Providing students with an opportunity to verbally process the information with a partner will also allow students to surface possible questions during the course of a student-to-student conversation. In having a discussion with a fellow student, it may be that each of the students in the pair, while listening to the teacher and taking notes earlier, heard and wrote down information that they interpreted or understood differently. Even a short conversation may lead one or both students to ask for clarification on a particular point.

Let's look at a scenario that plays out in, say, October, after several weeks of school. On a Tuesday afternoon, Mrs. McCord wants to introduce some new material related to her subject matter, and her lesson plan allows for thirty minutes out of a fifty-minute class period to do this. She has done the same thing in the past with a thirty-minute lecture and has followed that with a quiz (summative) a couple of days later, just to keep students on their toes and to see how they did—and by extension, how *she* did. She has noticed that the grades on those quizzes have tended to be low and that the students don't seem to grasp the key concept(s) contained in the information covered during the lectures. She has tried giving them an extra day or two to study, but to no avail. The scores peaked in mid-September and are now on a downward spiral. Since the students are not processing the information at home, Mrs. McCord decides to use another fifteen minutes to work some processing into the lesson and build in some time to check for understanding as well.

So with the introduction of this new material, she allows a total of forty-five minutes out of the fifty-five minute class period for the lesson, but decides to reduce the amount of teacher talk to a fifteen-minute mini-lecture, followed by fifteen minutes for reflective processing on their part and a final fifteen-minute block of time for her to ask questions that may help determine where they are in their understanding of the concepts and information without the pressure of a quiz grade. Once again, fifteen minutes for the mini-lecture, followed by fifteen minutes of student-to-student processing, capped off by fifteen minutes for questions (from and to Mrs. McCord).

On the Monday evening prior to Tuesday's lesson, Mrs. McCord comes up with a script for that fifteen-minute reflective processing session in the middle. She also identifies some upbeat music that she can play on her CD player to get them up and moving and to use during their sharing sessions. Her first period class enters that next morning, puts their homework papers in the proper bin, and opens their notebooks. Standing on a step stool in the front of the room, Mrs. McCord gets their attention, explains what they are about to do, and begins.

Direction 1   "Put your pen or pencil down!" (She checks to see this is done.)

Direction 2   "Stand behind your chair!" (She waits until everyone is standing.)

Direction 3   "Grab your notebook or the sheet on which you were taking notes and hold it up!" (She looks around to make certain everyone is holding up his or her notebook.)

Direction 4   "In five seconds, when I say go, take your notes, move to another part of the room, and find a partner who is not currently standing next to you or directly behind you!"

Direction 5   "Ready . . . Go!" (She plays some upbeat music while they move about the room. She then facilitates the process of finding a partner, and if there is an odd number of students in the room, she creates a trio.)

Direction 6   "In five seconds, when I say go, discuss with your partner or partners the notes you took. I'll check in with you in about five minutes. On the board are some questions to help guide your thinking." (She asks if there are *process-related* questions before proceeding.)

Direction 7   "Ready everyone . . . Go!" (She plays some more upbeat music that will allow students to have their discussions without being overheard by other pairs or trios. Then, stepping down from the step stool, she circulates around the room and listens to the conversations. During her progress around the classroom, she overhears two or three really good points made by students and quietly asks them if they will share those points with the whole class later on. She lets them go for the length of one song. As she circulates, she does not have to worry about the time because she recognizes when the song is almost done. She holds up her remote and hits the pause button, announcing that they still have fifteen seconds. When they resume talking for that final few seconds, she stands on the step stool once again.)

Direction 8   "Pause and look this way! Please thank your partner for sharing." (Pause.) "Return to your seats." (She plays more upbeat music while they move to their seats.)

Direction 9   "Tony, would you mind sharing what you and Cindy were talking about during your conversation?" (Mrs. McCord calls on Tony and the second student whom she asked to share. Next, after that discussion and maybe a total of fifteen or twenty minutes after the mini-lecture ended, *it is finally time to ask if there are questions!* She has a student record the questions on a chart or on the board. After having the class give a round of applause to the recorder, she *THEN begins to work her way through the charted questions.* Noticing that she is short on time, she pulls from the list two unanswered questions and asks them to write them down and do their best to answer them tonight for a continuation of the discussion tomorrow.)

So the first fifteen-minute segment of the lesson consisted of straight instruction while students took notes. The middle third was a blend of instruction and a simultaneous check for understanding using a standing pair-share activity. The last fifteen minutes was pretty much a check for understanding (formative assessment). Let's dissect the second and third segments of the lesson.

First, Mrs. McCord spent most of the time during the student-to-student conversations *listening to each of the pairs or trios in turn.* This gave her the perfect opportunity to eavesdrop and check for understanding. The original questions she had posted on the board gave them some focus, and their notes gave them additional information so that they were not relying totally on short-term memory. Second, once she had them return to their seats, she was able to get a class discussion going based on her own observations as she walked around the room, or on Tony's summarization of his conversation with Cindy, along with a comment from a second student she had asked to share. Third, she used the final fifteen minutes to ask some questions of her own and to surface some questions or misconceptions that may have arisen from the mini-lecture, note taking, and discussion. If she still wants to give a quiz on Thursday or Friday, it is a safe bet that their scores will be higher than when she simply relied on lecture and their own attempts at processing their notes at home.

Most importantly, perhaps, the students themselves were checking for understanding with their partners as they discussed the material. Their notes may have differed, and their take on the content may have diverged at various points. In these types of simultaneous conversations, students have the opportunity to assess their own understanding by comparing and contrasting it with the analysis of their partners.

Ramping Up Thinking and Peer-Assessing

Fisher and Frey (2007) cite a study by Vosniadou, Ioannides, Dimitrakopoulou, and Papademetriou (2001) which involves two groups of students taking part in a physics lesson.

> With one group of students, the researchers checked for understanding before moving on to the next part of the lesson. They did so by presenting students with a brief scenario and asking them to predict and explain the outcome. The other group participated in the exact same lesson but without any pauses to check for understanding. As you might expect, the findings clearly demonstrated that the first group had a significantly greater increase in post-test over pre-test performance on assessments of content knowledge. (p. 3)

Clearly, giving students time to talk with each other about content-related information, as Mrs. McCord did, will solidify their understanding and raise questions on their part that indicate they are engaged in the material. As we saw with the physics lesson, learning is enhanced when students have to do more than just recall facts and other information. Also, by moving around the room and listening to the student conversations, teachers have a wonderful opportunity to see what needs to be done, if anything, before moving on.

Questioning Techniques

I often paused during direct instruction long enough to ask a question. It might have begun like this, "Can anyone tell me . . . ?" Now, if Eddie heard me ask that question, he could rest assured that "anyone" did not include him. Mr. Nash had asked yet another question, and there were five or six students in the class whose hands shot up immediately. Eddie's wasn't one of them. He knew I was looking for the correct answer, and he also knew that someone in that small group of first-responders would take care of it . . . and give me the satisfaction of getting a "right answer" from someone. Thus, Eddie could safely hide in that class of thirty or so ninth graders.

There are ways to make certain that Eddie is on his toes at all times. One method is what Popham (2008) calls *random-response Q&A.* Instead of asking if anyone has the answer to whatever question is being asked, students are chosen at random to answer. "A good way to do this is to write each student's name on a tongue depressor or popsicle stick and select one from the collection after posing the question" (p. 59). Pausing to choose a name after asking the questions gives students time to think about possible answers. The great thing about this, according to Popham, "is that every student has an equal opportunity to be selected as the designated question answerer on all occasions" (p. 60). Not to put too fine a point on it, Eddie has no place to hide in such a structure. If this kind of random questioning is done frequently, he would do well to be prepared in the event the bell tolls for him.

Art Costa (2008) suggests another way to encourage students to engage in meaningful discussions and otherwise "set the conditions in which the student's interest is piqued" (p. 196). Instead of asking "Who can tell me . . . ? (a question that implies there is one right answer and the teacher is looking for someone who can come up with it), Costa suggests teachers begin with "What do we know about . . . ?" (p. 197). Beginning the query with *we* instead of *who* implies that everyone in the class may be fully capable of providing some input. The resulting discussion should give the teacher an idea of where everyone is related to the topic under consideration. Also, the notion that the teacher is not looking for that one right answer but is instead seeking input from many students in the class may encourage conversation and help students "develop a questioning attitude" (p. 197). The door is open for Eddie to contribute in this freewheeling discussion of the topic under consideration.

Having students stand and pair up for a discussion has more than one benefit. Sousa (2001) recommends that somewhere in a lesson, "students should be up and moving about, preferably talking about their new learning. Not only does the movement increase cognitive function, but it also helps students get rid of kinesthetic energy—the 'wiggles,' if you will—so they can settle down and concentrate later" (p. 231). Having discussed the information and, perhaps, worked together to answer some key questions, students will have a great deal more to think about when they do finally sit down.

Final Thoughts

Most teachers I know, and I include myself here, love to talk. If, however, we consider that our job is to find out where students are in their understanding of new information, then we must give *them* ample time to explain, summarize, elucidate, infer, wrestle with, and demonstrate in some way what *they* have come to know. This means that, as is so often the case in life, we must provide balance. While there will be plenty of opportunities for us to talk and for them to listen, we need to give the kids time to talk while we listen and observe. It is by listening and observing that we can gauge where they are in their academic journey and provide the feedback necessary for them to make adjustments as needed. Put another way, kids need to *do* in order to grow.

All of which brings us back to Eddie. In a classroom where periods of lecture and note-taking are followed by summative quizzes and tests, Eddie is pretty much on his own. If he disconnects during the lecture, takes poor notes, and does not process what little information he gleaned on his own, then he is not likely to do well on the quiz or test that will inevitably follow. If the teacher is utilizing a pacing guide, the results of the summative assessments are recorded and then Eddie, the teacher, and the rest of Eddie's classmates all move on. This very passive, largely summative cycle is expensive for Eddie and everyone else in the class, including the teacher who is *frustrated* with low student performance and with disengaged kids who are tired of watching the teacher work.

I have always thought that our job as educators is to help Eddie do something *today* he could not do *yesterday*. At every turn, we need to give him feedback and then provide opportunities for him "to act on the feedback—to refine, practice, and retry" (Tomlinson & McTighe, 2006, p. 79). If we as teachers live for the moment when the kids "get it," then Eddie is not the only one who may be excited about having taken that next step in his continuous improvement journey. We have the opportunity to be there when he gets it, and when he does, we understand once again why we went into teaching in the first place.

Formative assessment techniques that allow frequent checks and opportunities for constant adjustments in student performance are far cheaper in the long run than summative assessments that may have no lasting *positive* effect on Eddie's continuous improvement journey. If his summative quiz and test scores spiral downward week after week, it will have a negative impact on his (and the teacher's) confidence and motivation. If the frequent use of *formative* assessment techniques results in a steady increase in Eddie's summative scores, this will positively impact his confidence and motivation. This seems to me to be an extremely cost-conscious and cost-effective approach to managing process in the classroom.

All this, once again, is not to say that there is no place for summative assessments, which can provide teachers with needed data as to how they are doing. Teachers can work together on assessments that inform everyone concerned as to progress at a given point in time on the way to an individual or a common goal. O'Neill and Conzemius (2006) articulate this well:

> When common assessments, collaboratively developed by teams of teachers, are used both formatively (during learning, to promote learning) and summatively (at the end of learning, to evaluate learning), teachers get the added benefit of promoting student learning as well as their own learning. (p. 7)

Teachers, then, need to consider carefully the relative merits of both summative and formative assessments so that their use will provide students and teachers with vehicles for improvement in the short term (frequent formative assessments that provide students with necessary feedback) and in the long term (summative assessments that provide teachers with feedback).

In Chapter 7, we will take a look at the value of collaboration at all levels in the schoolhouse. Teaching can be but does not have to be a lonely profession. Administrators and other teachers can and should be trusted *investment partners* with whom much can be accomplished in the continuous improvement process. Sharing the inherent costs of investment with others in the organization simply makes good sense.

7

Enlisting Investment Partners

Mrs. Barnaby, a high school English teacher in her twelfth year in the profession, always wondered what went on in room 112. She would habitually head for the faculty lounge about ten minutes into second period (her prep), and she would occasionally linger next to the closed door of Ms. Stamford's room just long enough to catch the sound of music from inside. A glimpse through the narrow window often showed kids standing and sharing something with a partner or in a trio. Mrs. Barnaby would often shake her head in wonderment at what seemed to her to be a chaotic classroom. Ms. Stamford, a sophomore English teacher, was in her second year at the school and Mrs. Barnaby frankly knew little about her, except that control didn't appear to be her strong suit.

In January, the principal brought the staff together and announced that henceforth faculty meetings as information dumps would be outlawed. Such information as needed to be dispensed would be delivered via a short Friday newsletter and the time formerly spent on "administrivia" would be used to focus on instruction. At that first meeting in January, the principal distributed copies of Spark: The Revolutionary New Science of Exercise and the Brain, by John Ratey. The principal split the teachers into groups of ten. The groups were further subdivided into five pairs and Mrs. Barnaby found herself paired with Ms. Stamford—she of room 112.

Each pair took one of the first five chapters of Spark *and was then given the task of working together to first read and then report back to the group in February. Ms. Stamford volunteered her home for a meeting with Mrs. Barnaby one week hence, after both had read the chapter they had chosen—Chapter 1. During that subsequent meeting, Mrs. Barnaby asked Ms. Stamford about those frequent occasions when the kids in 112 were standing and sharing while music played in the background. Ms. Stamford laughed and explained that after she lectured or read to them from a story for a few minutes, she would stop, get the students on their feet in pairs or trios, and have them discuss what they had just heard.*

Ms. Stamford explained that this provided the students with a break, along with an opportunity to stand, move, and share content-related information. Ms. Stamford pointed out that the book Spark *lent credence to what she was doing because it underlined the importance of exercise as it relates to learning. She also shared that the kids loved getting up, moving, and sharing, once they got used to it, and that the reason she played music in the background as they talked was to provide a "cover" for the conversations, so that the kids could talk without being overheard. Ms. Stamford invited Mrs. Barnaby to come and visit during second period the next day.*

The two English teachers not only did a great job of presenting the material in Chapter 1 of Ratey's book, they also became friends, as did their families. Each of them picked up various instructional strategies from the other, and the two of them wound up presenting at a regional educational conference during the summer. They often marveled that they had spent well over two years in the same hallway without doing much more than saying hello a couple of times during the course of a week. It was not until the principal brought them together to look at instructional issues that they discovered the value of collaborating together and as part of larger groups within the high school faculty. Even though Mrs. Barnaby and Ms. Stamford were several years apart in age, they found they had much to learn from each other—with their students as the ultimate beneficiaries.

At the outset of my teaching career, in the early seventies, I was pretty much on my own. My students were provided with a history text. I was given a grade book, a class list, and a schedule; I ran with it. My classroom in those early years is best captured by Garmston and Wellman (1999) in their description of a traditional classroom: "Lectures, videos, reading from textbooks, note taking, and quizzes prevail. Students play out their part of the ritual, minimally complying with this production" (p. 26). They were speaking of "old ways of doing business in the classroom" (p. 26), and my classroom fit the description. Any personal reflection on my own performance as a young teacher came in the evenings when I looked back on the day's events; but such reflection was haphazard and did not have the benefit of the perspective of anyone other than myself. I did see other teachers in the faculty lounge—a fairly large room divided into smoking and nonsmoking sections—but attempts at collaboration for the purpose of sharing ideas or instructional strategies were, as I recall, rare.

My sense is that my experience in the early seventies was not at all unusual. Except for the smoking and nonsmoking faculty lounge, what I have described may still strike teachers today as familiar. The teacher and the long-distance runner have the loneliness of their pursuits in common. Many teachers, working basically on their own over many years, can become extremely proficient, supremely confident, highly knowledgeable, and demonstrably successful practitioners. Our fictitious teacher in the story that opened the chapter, Mrs. Barnaby, considered herself to be an excellent teacher. Yet she had her eyes opened when she began to work with Ms. Stamford and read the books and articles that were part of the regularly scheduled faculty sessions initiated by her principal. She soon began to take the time to read relevant material that had *not* been assigned and discovered a new, less-complacent and more self-reflective attitude toward teaching. The performance of professionals can always benefit from multiple perspectives and the feedback of colleagues.

Maeroff (1993) surfaces an uncomfortable truth obvious to anyone who has spent much time in education when he says that "teamwork, for almost any purpose, is foreign to most teachers. The measure of most teachers' success usually rests on how adept they are at working on their own" (p. 514). The physical isolation that originates in the "structure of school facilities and the schedules that dominate the school day," according to Hord and Sommers (2008), lead to the kind of "mental isolation" that is the norm in many school communities (p. 1). Teachers simply become used to working alone and may come to prefer it, something that makes it difficult for a principal or school leadership team to change direction and establish a culture of collegiality.

In this atmosphere, improvement efforts, according to Little (cited in Schmoker, 1999) are "limited to the boundaries of their own experience" (p. 12) as teachers continue to function, and maybe struggle, on their own without the benefit of multiple perspectives from colleagues. This tendency to go it alone is not without consequences.

In fact, a lack of collegial support is one among several reasons why a lack of job satisfaction leads to half our new teachers leaving the profession within five years (Woods & Weasmer, 2002, p. 186).

Teachers who have the benefit of the support of colleagues in the building are more likely to succeed. Schmoker (1999) states that "evidence for the benefits of collaboration, rightly conducted, are overwhelming" (p. 12). Regular school-wide collaborative sessions where successes and strategies can be shared are of some use and can certainly be of assistance to individual teachers, but Schmoker cautions that to be of real value, teamwork in the schoolhouse must include the setting of goals that will help drive instruction: "Without explicit learning goals, we are simply not set up and organized for improvement, for results" (p. 23). Administrators and teachers involved in collaborative planning should make certain that challenging goals are part of the overall improvement process. The end game, though, is not simply setting goals, but making certain that classroom application is part of the process. Without this logical next step, the original collaborative planning will not have been cost-effective and will show little in the way of a return on investment.

There is another distinct benefit from collaboration in the school building. As we saw with Mrs. Barnaby and Ms. Stamford, whose teaming on a specific assignment led to a long-lasting friendship that involved their families, teachers have much to learn from each other. Although collaborative sessions will probably take place at school on a regular basis, there is some benefit to getting off campus on occasion. Maeroff (1993) said that a group of high school teachers made the decision to meet on "neutral ground, not subject to the departmental demarcations and removed from the pecking order that overlays interactions in the typical school building" (p. 73). A new teacher who finds that he is increasingly becoming part of a dynamic and positive school community is, presumably, far more likely to continue his career as an educator beyond that critical first year.

Cooperation at the District Level

I have always thought that school districts can learn much from each other. Just as we encourage teachers to observe other classrooms close to home, we should take the opportunity to visit other districts to see what they are doing that is powerful and effective. There is much to be learned out there that will benefit our teachers and students. Fullan (2005) suggests that both school and district leaders should not only commit themselves to "create learning communities from within, but also learning from and contributing to learning outside their jurisdictions. It is through the latter that people increase their system-thinking awareness and impact—an impact that is local and beyond" (p. 84). Districts that are further along on the continuous improvement highway have much to share by way of helping neighboring systems avoid the mistakes and pitfalls they have already experienced.

In the late nineties, a group of teachers, instructional coordinators, principals, and staff developers from the Virginia Beach City Public Schools drove to North Carolina to observe teachers and students in the Craven County Schools. The district superintendent and his leadership team had lunch with us and made us feel entirely welcome before we even ventured out beyond the district office. During the course of an afternoon and the next morning, we observed many classrooms at all levels. The classrooms we observed were those of teachers who had created effective learning communities and where student achievement was extraordinarily high. The students we observed were actively engaged in their own learning, and teachers and students alike operated at a high level of enthusiasm and performance. I still have a photograph of a third-grade girl who was *leading her classmates* in a discussion of author technique in a language arts lesson using a fishbone diagram and excellent facilitation skills. Reading and math scores were high wherever we went, and the teachers and students we observed were undoubtedly excited about and satisfied with what they were accomplishing. Our trip was a truly amazing experience, but the real power came not in the classroom visits but on the trip home.

We had driven two school district vans to and from North Carolina, and the drive home took several hours. This gave us time to reflect on what we had seen and, more important, what it meant for us as a school district. Everyone in those two vans had different perspectives on what we had observed. Each of us saw something different, even though we may have been in the same classrooms. The great thing about the ride home that day was that we never stopped asking questions, sharing ideas, offering insights, and taking the time—without distractions—to consider the implications and applications of what we had seen. It was an informal process, to be sure, but it was nevertheless refreshing and supremely motivating—and it was powerful evidence of what can be done when teachers, principals, and central office coordinators put their collective minds together in pursuit of continuous improvement.

Building Leadership Capacity

Reason and Reason (2007, September) affirm the importance of teacher leadership in building leadership capacity. They highlight the importance of a *classroom focus* for collaborative efforts in the schoolhouse: "Giving input on new administrative policies and helping the principal make key management decisions are important activities, but the most essential work in school doesn't take place in the principal's office" (p. 36). Leadership teams composed of teachers might take a look at what students need, what sacred cows can be discarded in favor of what will have more impact, what can make a difference in dealing with the community at large, and how teachers in the same department can learn to work collegially (p. 38). These bottom-up improvement efforts involve teachers asking and answering questions collaboratively, and what they do and decide should directly impact students.

As they move along the pathway in the journey to developing a collaborative culture, teachers emerging from an isolationist past should begin to realize "that their competence is directly and indivisibly linked to the competence of the system" (Zmuda, Kuklis, & Kline, 2004). In an *isolationist* culture, effective change comes in fits and starts. In a *collaborative* culture, change is much more likely to be permanent because the search for what is needed and what works is built into the system. Administrators need to facilitate the move toward a school-wide collaborative culture while developing a common vision that will help make certain that all the continuous improvement efforts are aligned.

It is possible that a school with a faculty of 124 teachers and administrators will have 124 different ideas of where the school should be headed. This can result in wasted energy as administrators and teachers go full speed in different, and often diametrically opposed, directions. Blankstein puts it this way: "Without a common vision, decisions are made randomly. At best, policies, procedures, and programs will lack unity and fail to adequately support one another. At worst, they will actually work at cross purposes" (p. 77). The lack of a shared and focused commitment toward a common goal is undoubtedly *expensive in the extreme*. Only a truly collaborative culture that relies on the collective and synergistic power of its stakeholders can move relentlessly toward the attainment of a common and well-defined set of goals and expectations.

Zmuda, Kuklis, and Kline (2004) recommend the collection and analysis of data as part of a collective effort to "inform the staff about the gaps between the shared vision and the current reality so they can produce a collective mandate for change that is in alignment with their core beliefs." Moreover, a staff that may be skeptical of the efficacy of top-down professional development mandates may emerge from their own analysis of the collected data a great deal "more invested in the staff development plan" (p. 104).

Involving Students in the Process

It is in the interest of every stakeholder in every school to begin the process of shifting the culture from one of teacher isolation to one of collaborative improvement efforts grounded firmly in the shared vision and core beliefs of the organization. No individual stakeholder, it could be argued, has a bigger stake in improving instruction and school climate than the students themselves. Mitra (2008) states that while student involvement outside the classroom is normally limited to extracurricular activities (dances, pep rallies), research indicates that getting students involved in school improvement efforts "can actually improve teachers' classroom practice" (p. 20).

At Whitman High School in California, for example, Mitra (2008) reports that students were included in school improvement efforts in part by forming focus groups that explored, among other things, new instructional strategies being developed by teachers in the school. "Students talked about specific modifications to instruction that would help them master content, drawing on the information about multiple intelligences that adults had shared with them" (p. 23). The Whitman experience demonstrated how "including student voice in reform efforts can strengthen schools" (p. 24).

Making It Happen

Efforts at developing a collaborative culture need the support of the school administration and will be unlikely to succeed if such assistance is not forthcoming. In fact, we have seen that the tradition of teacher isolation is a powerful force that may slow or bring to a halt the efforts of individuals or small groups among the faculty who attempt to move a culture from isolationist to functionally collaborative. Schmoker (1999) charges district administrators with the responsibility of providing deliberate staff development planning and decries its absence as "one of the most alarming realities of education in our time" (p. 116). It is up to administrators to provide the time necessary—and for teachers to take advantage of the time afforded—to work together in pursuit of meaningful and substantial instructional improvement.

Although district and building administrators need to be actively involved in the development of a professional learning community (PLC), "no school has ever made progress toward becoming a PLC until some of its members took steps to make it happen" (Eaker, DuFour, & DuFour, 2002, p. 7). Warning against waiting for someone else to do something, Eaker, DuFour, and DuFour (2002) encourage members of school communities to serve as catalysts in the cause of school improvement:

> Principals have helped create PLCs in their schools despite indifference from the central office. Department chairpersons have been successful in helping their departments function as a learning community in a school that does not. Individual teachers have banded together to demonstrate the power of a collaborative team in schools where most teachers continue to work in isolation. (pp. 7–8)

Teachers can begin not by waiting for something to happen, but by being proactive in first opening their classroom doors and making contact with other teachers in the building with whom they can work on collaborative projects such as interdisciplinary units or the development of departmental goals and common assessments. Teachers can begin to observe each other's classes, giving specific feedback in certain areas and learning much that can be transferred to the observer's classroom. Groups of teachers can collaborate on book talks and find and discuss the available research on a given topic related to education. A proactive teacher will find much to do in collaboration with colleagues in the schoolhouse and in the district that will benefit the continuous improvement process of teachers and students alike.

Following are some other suggestions that may help teachers and administrators work together collaboratively to facilitate progress and innovation in the building:

Redesign Faculty Meetings

Faculty meetings that are often little more than opportunities to pass along information to staff can be turned into occasions where teachers can participate in discussions of learning-centered issues, take an in-depth look at relevant data, and work on problems confronting the school community. Former principal Joanne Rooney (2006) transformed her faculty meetings from information sessions to "gatherings filled with creative collaboration and teacher learning" (p. 91). In time, Rooney's agenda as a principal shifted from a position at the front of the meetings to the end and "faculty meetings became, in actuality, *faculty* meetings" (p. 91). Rooney moved to the periphery as teachers became more comfortable with running the show.

Work With Substitute Teachers

Many current teachers and administrators spent time as substitute teachers before receiving a contract for a permanent teaching position. Anyone who has substitute taught over the years knows just how difficult that can be. In many school districts, the training program for substitutes amounts to "Hang in there!" We have them complete some paperwork, tell them to stay out of trouble, give them a list of things to do and not do . . . and into the fray they go. The ranks of substitute teachers are often replete with college students, recent college graduates in search of teaching jobs, those who may be seeking a career change from whatever they are currently doing to teaching full time, and those who simply need something to do until they begin a new job or get settled in the community. For any and all of these people, substitute teaching can be an imposing and frightening experience *for which they are most likely completely unprepared.*

My suggestion is that substitute teachers would be a lot more effective if teachers and administrators worked together to meet with them frequently and do some problem solving aimed at making them feel at home in the building, acknowledging their importance, and increasing their effectiveness. Most schools have a solid core of several substitute teachers who are in the building frequently. It seems to me that involving them in the shared vision and letting them avail themselves of some professional development opportunities would be time and money well spent. Teachers can take the lead here by making substitutes feel welcomed and wanted.

A permanent working group composed of teachers, administrators, and veteran substitute teachers could meet once a month to identify and discuss issues that affect everyone. For example, the team could come up with a folder that contains critical information related to that building that can be copied and placed on the top of the lesson plans and other classroom-specific information. For example, if there is a school-wide restroom policy, substitutes need to know what it is. That folder could also contain a sheet that outlines procedures and processes unique to that classroom teacher. For example, the folder could contain information on how the regular classroom teacher normally gets the attention of the students; knowing that three hand claps is the accepted (and effective) way to get everyone's attention is an essential ingredient to a successful day for the substitute and the kids.

I well remember the angst I felt when I was ill or on leave, wondering which substitute teacher had been in my classroom and how it had gone. If teachers and administrators can invest the time in collaborative, substantive dialogue with substitute teachers, my sense is that mutual issues, problems, and questions can be dealt with to the satisfaction of all concerned. In short, substitutes need not be taken for granted and teachers can easily take the lead here by working collaboratively with all concerned to make things run smoothly whenever teachers are out of the classroom.

District-level administrators can do their part by providing professional development for substitute teachers that will (1) clarify the instructional goals and shared vision of the district, (2) provide instructional strategies that can be used by substitute teachers when lesson plans are unclear or come up short in terms of time, and (3) make substitute teachers feel that they are truly part of the overall plan for educational excellence.

Tapping Into Untapped Resources

Everyone in the school community should be involved in the learning process, and my suggestion is that time and collaborative effort be devoted to making sure that all stakeholders are truly involved. I was once in an elementary school where everything in the school came to an abrupt halt while everyone in the building devoted thirty minutes to reading something . . . anything. There were hundreds of people in the building, but one could have heard the proverbial pin drop. The silence was deafening, and it was wonderful. Students, administrators, counselors, teachers, teacher assistants, office associates, custodians—no one was exempt from silent reading. Someone once said that if you are not modeling what you are teaching, you are teaching something else. The adults in this school were modeling what they were teaching; needless to say this habit of reading for a half hour every day paid off in reading scores, too. They tapped into the human resources in the building and put a collective face on excellence, commitment, and shared vision that was palpable, even to a visitor.

There is a (true) story I often tell about a custodian who was walking down the hallway near the office at the end of the school day. Walking in the opposite direction was an elementary student who was reading a book as she walked, oblivious to all around her. The custodian asked her what she was reading. When she showed him the book, he asked if she would like to read it to him. She said yes and so the two of them sat on a bench near the office and this young student read to the custodian. My guess is that nowhere in his job description for building custodian was it written that listening to a student read out loud was something he should do. My sense is that there was *nothing* he did that day that was more important than sitting on that bench and listening to that story.

Teachers can take the lead in tapping untapped resources in the school community. Meg Bozzone (1996) relates the story of an elementary school in Delaware "where the joyful cohesiveness of the faculty and staff envelops you like a warm blanket on a frosty night" (p. 54). Cafeteria workers at this school share the vision and "point to a map hanging above the lunch line and ask first graders who are studying European countries, 'Where in the world is Italy?'" (p. 54). If everyone in the building understands the shared vision, then, like the custodian and the cafeteria workers, they can move beyond what their job description entails and make a difference in ways unrelated to their normal duties.

Teachers can make a concerted effort to build a collegial atmosphere in the schoolhouse, and they don't need to wait for orders from above to do this. Teachers can approach administrators and explain what they would like to do in order to capture the collective positive energy from every adult in the building in order to benefit the kids they are all there to serve.

Identifying and Sharing Strengths

As human beings, we each have our own talents and strengths. For example, I am strong in communicative skills, but I am not particularly analytical. When I am working as the member of an ad hoc group or formal committee, I'm extremely comfortable sharing my views and taking a lively part in the discussion. Also, I can come to a conclusion on something fairly quickly in an attempt to move things along. Analytical people want to see the research before making a decision and insist on the soundness of the theories being expounded. Analytical people "search for patterns and connections" (Liesveld &

Miller, 2005, p. 76). An analytical teammate will challenge the group's thinking, and what results will have the benefit of that careful and unhurried analysis.

When working collaboratively to solve problems and make important decisions, administrators and teacher leaders would do well to diversify membership on groups or committees in terms of the members' individual talents and strengths. As mentioned above, it is critical to have at least one group member who will ask the tough questions as the process goes forward. If the committee is dealing with instructional issues, including someone who has command of Internet sites and resources would be paramount. Having someone who can facilitate the meetings in order to ensure that things move along smoothly would also be prudent. Without a facilitator, group discussion can soon digress, become aimless, and turn negative. The composition of committees and groups, then, becomes more than simply drawing names from a hat. Administrators and teacher leaders need to think carefully about the various strengths that potential group members will bring to the table.

Classroom Support

Harrison and Killion (2007) identify ten roles of teacher leaders, all of which are instruction-focused and one of which has teacher leaders working "inside classrooms to help teachers implement new ideas, often by demonstrating a lesson, coteaching, or observing and giving feedback" (p. 75). Two other related teacher-leader roles identified by Harrison and Killion include sharing instructional resources and assisting other teachers in the implementation of teaching strategies, and they are careful to point out that "whether these roles are assigned formally or shared informally, they build the entire school's capacity to improve" (p. 74).

The key here is for schools to take a systematic and relentless approach to providing the kind of classroom support necessary to improve instruction and accomplish the other goals that are tied to the mission and vision of the school. Without the kind of collective effort to provide support for new *and* veteran teachers, this classroom-level support will be hit-and-miss and dependent on the teachers providing the support staying in the building over time. If those few teachers providing instructional assistance retire or leave to work in another building, their innovation and improvement folder will go with them.

Final Thoughts

If, as Blankstein concludes in a chapter on collaborative teaming, "building collaborative teams is a difficult but necessary component of school success" (p. 14), administrators and teachers alike must open the doors to offices and classrooms, step out into the hallway, and embrace a collective commitment to a relentless pursuit of excellence that will benefit students and every other member of the school community.

For their part, teachers need to be confident in their abilities to take leadership roles and work collaboratively with their peers and administrators. "For teachers to assume these leadership roles, a critical additional element is for teachers to see themselves as leaders" (McCombs & Whisler, 1997, p. 161). This can be difficult in cultures where "Just tell me what you want me to do!" is deeply ingrained in the collective psyche of teachers and staff. Administrators need to empower teachers to move beyond the role of follower and into important positions of leadership in the school community.

Chapter 8 provides an opportunity to explore the issue of relevance as it pertains to students and learning. In an age where teachers are no longer the primary source of information available to students, the very role of teachers must change. Helping students make sense and meaning of what has become a torrent of information is critical to them as they enter the workforce and deal with an increasingly complex world. Helping students learn how to think critically, ask questions, communicate effectively, solve problems, and make decisions may well be our most important job as educators at every level and in every classroom.

8

Ramping Up Relevance

A teacher once told me that his job was to present the information to his students; if they did not "get it," that was not his problem. Those in education who still cling to the notion that teachers are "presenters of information" need to understand that students have access to sources of information not dreamed of when I was in school in the fifties and sixties, or when I started teaching in the early seventies. Teachers today are simply one among almost limitless sources of information. Students are awash in facts and data, available at their fingertips twenty-four hours a day. Indeed, students would have to work hard to avoid being inundated with information in the twenty-first century.

This means that teachers who decide to simply add to this plethora of incoming data risk becoming not only ineffective, but irrelevant. It means that teachers can't simply make themselves one more source of information; instead they must assist students who are trying to make sense and meaning of it all. Garner (2007) articulates this well: "Because information in today's fast-paced, multimedia world is doubling every few months, it is crucial that our students learn how to learn—how to 'figure out how to figure out'—so that they can make sense of the unfamiliar information they encounter on a daily basis" (pp. xv–xvi). If the *process* is one of doing that which helps students construct meaning out of multitudinous and seemingly disparate pieces of information, then teachers can best assist students by serving as facilitators of that process.

In this expanded role, teachers need to help students think critically, question methodically, solve problems, and communicate their feelings and understandings effectively. Teachers must constantly plan, evaluate, reflect, and adjust how they do what they do in order to be relevant in a world where circumstances have changed dramatically. This includes understanding that students today understandably resist the passivity of many traditional classrooms.

When I first began my teaching career, I mimicked my own high school teachers and college professors by relying on lecture as a delivery vehicle for information. I talked while my students listened and took notes, and (I hoped) spent time after school, in the evening, or on weekends processing information. A second major source of information for my students was the history textbook, the structure of which encouraged me to assign a small section of reading each night. Each section concluded with several questions my students were required to answer and return as homework the following day. From my students' perspective, other than my lecture and their personal copy of the history textbook, the only other sources of information available to them (and to me, for that matter) consisted of the print media stored in local libraries. By today's standard, it was a simple and relatively uncomplicated world in which information sources were few.

Set aside for the moment that lecturing and assigning sections of the text on a daily basis did not work well then; it is simply irrelevant today as a single mode of instruction. This does not mean that there is no place for lecture, but a short ten-minute lecture can and should be followed by an opportunity *in class* for students to process the information. If the technology is available in the building, students can extend their own learning by searching the web for additional information, pictures, videos, and commentaries on the subject at hand. Students who have computers and access to the internet at home are constantly in an extending-their-own-learning mode. Anything they might want to know about is at their fingertips in short order.

I was in an elementary library recently where the books had been relegated to shelves around the perimeter and there were dozens of computers on tables in the center of the room. The computers in that library are in constant use and the information available electronically is current and therefore more relevant to the kids at the keyboards. Students can find information much more quickly with a mouse and a keyboard than they can by visiting the library stacks, and the information available electronically is up to date. Not only are teachers not the sole source of information today, they are not even the most important source of information for their students.

For a former history teacher like me who plodded with my students in lockstep through the textbook, the idea of instant information that is constantly updated and refreshed at the click of a mouse is truly amazing. In the future, kids with four heavy textbooks in their backpacks will, I am quite certain, gladly shed their burden as electronic technology continues to work its way into classrooms all over America. That twenty-pound backpack could be replaced by a data stick that a high school student can carry around with him on his key ring.

During the campaigns leading up to the 2008 national election, I became a virtual information junkie. I found that I could visit any one of a dozen Web sites and see text and video literally only minutes old and available to me any time day or night. This baby boomer who was once satisfied watching Chet Huntley, David Brinkley, or Walter Cronkite deliver the news in a rather sedate and straightforward fashion, now craves a television screen with the images of six or seven pundits, reporters, and experts, along with *at least* one crawling message across the bottom. I can Google anything at any time, and the world is literally at my fingertips and just one or two clicks away. Though this remarkable personal transformation is a revelation to me, *it is all the current generation knows.* I used to send my students to the library to do research. Today, such research is at most student's fingertips at school or at home, and the library of yesteryear is now called a media center where the media specialist in charge facilitates process, but is no more the sole repository of information than is the classroom teacher. Kids don't want to inquire about something; they want to click, search, and locate information on their own.

Early in my career, I remember walking by a secondary classroom where the lights were out, the shades were drawn, and the students were asleep. The take-up reel on a 16mm movie projector provided the only sound in the room as it thwap-thwap-thwapped away, waiting for the teacher to shut the movie projector off. He couldn't do that, however, because he was also asleep. If the idea of students sitting still for fifty minutes watching an educational video and getting something from it was unlikely thirty years ago, it is almost laughable today. Few students of the early twenty-first century can sit still and watch a screen containing many talking heads and little in the way of fast-paced action sequences or split-screen images. Yet there are educational videos twenty and thirty years old still being shown in classrooms all over the country.

Today's students, by the time they get to high school, have completed all the worksheets they want to complete, watched all the decades-old videos they want to watch, and have sat through all the forty-minute lectures they want to hear. Being a passive observer is honestly not something that appeals to students. I have heard teachers complain that kids today do not want to learn. It is not that they don't want to learn; the truth is that sitting still listening to the teacher or watching a video is not something they can do for long without losing interest and going somewhere else in their minds. Those same kids will spend hours in front of a computer screen accessing information and communicating with friends and with other people, many of whom they have never actually met. In school, students may be passive observers because they *have* to. When they leave the building, they become active learners because they *want* to.

A Bias Toward Action

Brown (2000) contrasts the learning process of older generations with the youth of today, who, as he notes, have a "bias toward action" (p. 14).

> My generation tends not to want to try things unless or until we already know how to use them. If we don't know how to use some appliance or software, our instinct is to reach for a manual or take a course or call up an expert. Believe me, hand a manual or suggest a course to 15 year olds and they think you are a dinosaur. They want to turn the thing on, get in there, muck around, and see what works. Today's kids get on the Web and link, lurk, and watch how other people are doing things, then try it themselves. (p. 14)

This tendency toward action means that teachers, as part of being effectively proactive, need to understand this aversion to passivity and plan accordingly. Teachers who do not do this will pay a heavy price, no matter the grade level. I once observed an elementary classroom where the students sat still for thirty minutes, listening to the teacher and writing on a worksheet. I watched their body language closely during that time, and I can report that as the minutes ticked by they became increasingly restless. They needed to get up and move, talk, or just *do something*. Some of the kids began to act out and the teacher had to deal with it; this was the result of being largely reactive and waiting on events as the kids themselves reacted to having to sit for a half hour. Planning for that particular lesson was easy, but it came with a heavy price in the execution.

By contrast, in another elementary classroom, I saw the kids move in a purposeful fashion at least three times in thirty minutes. They stood to the sound of music; they used that same upbeat song to get into pairs (and cheerily sang the words to the song while doing so); they shared information while music was playing; they moved to different seats with different partners to take part in another round of sharing . . . and they loved it. The fact that there was music playing while they talked did not bother them at all. They also worked quietly on some individual work during that half hour, but that was the exception rather than the norm. Getting up, sitting down, sharing with a partner, singing the lyrics to the song, and working individually (and quietly) was all part of that teacher's instructional mosaic . . . and it worked. Those students moved, talked, listened, laughed, sang, sat, shared . . . and learned. The teacher had done her homework and understood that this bias for action on the part of her students had to be accommodated in her planning. Being proactive by predicting that the kids needed to move, talk, and process information during the lesson paid dividends in the end. Her role during the execution of the lesson plan was that of process facilitator.

Teachers as Process Facilitators

In a world where cable and satellite companies make available hundreds of channels and the Internet makes the amount of information at our fingertips almost limitless, the idea that a classroom teacher's job is simply to provide information, therefore, makes little sense. What is far more relevant in today's world is for teachers to become proficient at showing students how to process and make meaning out of the glut of information available. The most important role of a teacher today may be that of process facilitator, working with students to develop twenty-first-century skills such as thinking critically, solving problems, making decisions, and communicating effectively. In life and in the world of work, where teamwork is increasingly more important, these skills are critical to success. In an electronic world where the amount of information is overwhelming, teachers would do well to provide time in the classroom to let students *process* that information, ask questions, deliberate, disagree, analyze, synthesize, and otherwise make sense of it all.

Human beings need time to think about and talk about new information in an attempt to construct meaning. An example of what can happen when people are given time to do this processing in class comes from the world of business. Brown (2000) relates how a Stanford professor, teaching an engineering course in which several Hewlett-Packard engineers were enrolled, discovered that many of the H-P students were transferred during the semester and were therefore unable to attend the remaining classes. The professor had the course sessions videotaped and sent the tapes to the students for viewing.

Rather than simply view the tapes in their entirety while taking notes, however, the H-P engineers would roll the tape for a few minutes and then "talk about what they'd just seen, ask each other if there were any questions or ambiguities, and resolve them on the spot" (p. 17). What they did, in other words, was to construct "their own meaning of the material" (p. 17). The test results showed that those who finished the course in this way did better than those who were in the actual classes week after week. Here is clear evidence that short periods of lecture or video supported by thoughtful discussion and opportunities to clarify misunderstandings can lead to real understanding.

Life Is Not a Multiple-Choice Test

In the multiple-choice assessments that predominate in this era of standardized testing, students are safe in the knowledge that the right answer is there among the four options. It is a matter of either knowing the correct answer or taking an educated guess. The race for good grades on these end-of-year tests tempts many teachers to simply forego the teaching of necessary skills in search of the shortest route to higher test scores. This is unfortunate for many reasons, not the least of which is that life is not a multiple-choice test. Life in general and the workplace in particular are far more complicated, and the skills needed to succeed cannot be thrust aside for the sake of good test performance. This is not to say that the information tested in the state and local tests is not important, but to the extent that such results do not correlate to success in life and in the workplace, the headlong rush for high scores should not displace that which is necessary when students graduate from high school.

Business leaders today increasingly want employees who "know how to innovate, solve problems, and work with people from other cultures as much as they need to know algebra and U.S. history"

(Gewertz, 2008, p. 21). Time spent preparing students for tests takes away from time that could be used to show them how to solve problems—something that they will need in life and in the workplace. Hannaford (2005) articulates the conflict between constant testing and a need to

> ... see problem solving in a larger context. ... [This stress of constant testing] turns education into a numbers game where competition, rather than cooperation, is encouraged and information is not moved to applicability or creative thought. If we can advance to an education that balances memory and thinking, and honors each person's learning processes, agile learners with valuable thinking tools can emerge. (p. 215)

Wagner (2008b) relates the story of a business executive who told him that in hiring employees he looked for those who were capable of asking good questions and engaging customers. Said this executive, "I want people who can engage in good discussion—who can look me in the eye and have a give and take" (p. 20). In his book *The Global Achievement Gap*, Wagner (2008a) quotes Karen Bruett, in charge of strategic business development at Dell and past president of the Partnership for 21st Century Skills, who explains that work today is "defined by the task or problem you and your team are trying to solve or the end goal you want to accomplish" (p. 15). Teams, as Bruett points out, "have to figure out the best way to get there—the solution is not prescribed" (p. 15). In a modern workplace, where collaboration may be the norm, communication and problem-solving skills are critical. It would seem to be necessary, then, that schools take the time to incorporate these life- and work-related skills into the curriculum.

The Coexistence of Content and Process

To say that these performance skills are needed in today's workplace is not to imply that math and science, to name two critical subject areas, are not important. I am not suggesting that school districts simply discard old curricula and replace them with something totally new. I am suggesting that there is room in the curriculum of any grade level for the introduction of those performance skills that are becoming increasingly important in a global society, and in ways explored and demonstrated in this book. A student who learns to ask questions, think critically, and communicate effectively is in a much better position to learn the content. It is therefore relevant to help students learn performance skills that will assist them in understanding course content and, for that matter, all the information with which they are inundated during most of their waking hours.

The idea is to use the content to teach process and, simultaneously, use process to learn content. The task for teachers is to figure out ways to go into more depth in critical content areas, as Mrs. McCord did with her students in Chapter 6. She did not get rid of lecture; she reduced the amount of lecture in order to find time for her students to process information, formulate questions, and then ask those questions or answer hers. Mrs. McCord understood and honored her students' propensity for action. She realized that kids have to move and kids have to talk, and she enlisted these tendencies as allies in her quest to help students sift through the constant flow of data and construct meaning. Once again, it is not about the *what* as much as it is about the *how* of teaching.

What applies to lecture can be applied to the use of videos. Teachers really don't need to show an entire thirty-minute educational video if a five-minute lecture can segue into a four-minute video segment that helps explain or enhance the lecture. Both the lecture and the video segment can be followed by a paired conversation where students are able to process what they have learned and surface questions with each other that they can later raise with the teacher. Not only do the students get a chance to solidify their knowledge of the course content contained in the lecture and the video segment, they are practicing the art of conversation—something that will stand them in good stead with employers who expect them to confidently present a viewpoint and ask good questions as part of a team working to give their company an advantage in the global market.

Cost-Effective Use of Time

In economic terms, given the fact that the time spent with students is finite, how can teachers become cost-effective in their investment of that time? Turning lectures into mini-lectures, reducing a thirty-minute video to a four-minute segment, and eliminating worksheets (for which your students will thank you) will provide the time to go into more depth in the twin areas of content and process. Students who enjoy the learning process in school will not, I believe, hesitate to extend that learning at home—and on their own time. Students who have access to a vast array of information sources and are assisted by teachers who understand their role as facilitators of process will succeed on any standardized test sent their way. More important, they will succeed in life and in the workplaces of today that require skill sets related to communication, collaboration, critical thinking, and problem solving.

Students who recognize the utility of those skills and who become proficient in those areas will be much better off and ultimately more successful in school. Moreover, a student who by the age of fifteen or sixteen has received considerable practice in those skill areas and recognizes their importance to his or her future is, I would argue, less likely to drop out of high school. *If he sees the relevance of what he is learning,* he may well decide to stay in school and parlay his degree and his newly acquired skill set into a job.

I have stressed the importance of these skills for the workplace here, but Wagner (2008a) states that mastering these skills will also help our young people succeed in life. The skills are "what we all need in order to be contributing citizens in a vibrant democracy—and to confront the challenges and make the changes that we must for a better future for our children" (p. 271). Life has always been *and will always be* about thinking critically, solving problems, communicating effectively, and making solid decisions that directly affect individuals and families. These skills are also sought after by employers looking for an edge in the global economy.

Beland (2007) affirms that oral communication, teamwork/ collaboration, and ethics/social responsibility are three of the most sought-after skills as reported in a 2006 survey of four-hundred human resource professionals conducted by the Partnership for 21st Century Skills. She reports that students at Eleanor Roosevelt High School (in Maryland) "are taking part in a new program that integrates social and emotional learning into the high school curriculum" (p. 68). Beland makes the point that students who do not possess these skills "will be hard-pressed to fulfill their potential, whether they pursue post-secondary education or head straight to the world of work" (p. 69). At Eleanor Roosevelt High School, classroom teachers "foster discussion skills that help students actively and respectfully listen to their peers" (p. 70).

This idea of having a classroom discussion or leading students in a series of structured conversations in a safe atmosphere is critical in the development of these relationship- and communication-related skills. One challenge is that the sheer number of occasions where students can have the kinds of conversations that help build relationships has diminished over the decades. Opportunities for conversation that were once available as a matter of course have diminished with the passing of decades as our daily habits and routines have adjusted to the electronic age.

A New Reality

Dinner, when I was growing up in the fifties and early sixties, was an event. One did not miss dinner; dinner took precedence over other activities. Dinner often took place in the dining room or at the kitchen table and consisted of children and adults eating and having conversations. Meals of any kind and at any time of day were opportunities for the kind of conversations that are rare today. On those occasions when we did go out to dinner, it was another opportunity for oral communication. When I went next door to my friends' house, once dinner was over, the conversation moved to the kitchen where, as a guest, I had a choice—I could wash or dry (the dishes). Here was another twenty minutes or so that extended the conversation from the dinner table to the kitchen. During the course of a week there were, therefore, many hours devoted as a matter of course to conversations that allowed baby boomers to become comfortable with oral communication and, specifically, confident in speaking with adults.

My purpose in relaying this bit of nostalgia is not to pine for the good old days, but to point out that much has changed. I recently visited a restaurant with over forty video screens, some offering live sports events and others offering opportunities for patrons to interact with the screens. As I ate lunch in that restaurant one day, a group of five entered and sat at a table in the center of the room. There were three boys of various ages in the group and two adults whom I took to be their parents. Two of the boys, along with the father, gazed at the various screen images and programs around the restaurant, while the youngest boy, not content with what was on offer on forty-plus screens, played a video game and focused intently on his hand-held model. While the father and the boys spent their time distracted by one screen or another, the mother spent a good deal of the meal talking on her cell phone. With all these distractions at the ready, along with music loud enough to discourage talking, it did not surprise me that there was little in the way of conversation at that nearby table.

The technology on which we have come to rely has its price, and it means teachers are opening their classroom doors to students who have been rewired. The hours I spent as a child taking part in fairly structured and always frequent conversations outside of the classroom have been displaced in too many cases by self-indulgent activities that preclude those conversations. If kids are no longer having long conversations at the dinner table, in the restaurant, or in the family car, then all eyes turn to the classroom teacher for intervention and support.

Communication and Socialization Imperatives

If students are going to develop the kinds of communication and socialization skills necessary to succeed in the workplace of the twenty-first century, they need to practice those skills in the classroom. This means that teachers must provide opportunities for students to engage in conversations with other students, something that requires empathetic listening. Active, or empathetic, listening requires us to pay attention, to focus, and to empathize—even though we may not agree with what our partner is saying. Costa (2008) says we need to get students to quit laughing at or putting down another student's ideas.

> We wish students to learn to hold in abeyance their own values, judgments, opinions, and prejudices in order to listen to and entertain another person's thoughts. This is a very complex skill requiring the ability to monitor one's own thoughts while, at the same time, attending to one's partner's words. . . . A good listener tries to understand what the person is saying. In the end he may disagree sharply, but because he disagrees, he wants to know exactly what he is disagreeing with. (p. 33)

Teachers need to provide plenty of opportunities for students to face each other and practice the listening skills that will help them become better communicators and better understand the perspectives and positions of other students. When the entire class is engaged in structured conversations where students practice both speaking and listening skills, everyone benefits. Lipton and Wellman (2000) maintain that engaging "in shared problem solving, public discussion and thinking aloud increases individual learner's capacities, adds to the collective knowledge of the class and demonstrates the importance of shared information processing and shared skills refinement" (p. 6). Once students are comfortable with sharing with a partner or in a group, subject-area content can be introduced into the mix.

Teachers need to make students aware of the role and impact of body language, facial expressions, tone of voice, and eye contact in becoming better at oral communication skills. Teachers also need to make sure that structured student-to-student conversations are included in daily planning. With practice, students can become used to having these paired and group conversations with topics comfortable to them (favorite movies, meals, books, vacations, pastimes) before introducing course content. For example, only when students have adjusted to and become proficient with having student-to-student conversations about something with which they are totally familiar would a social studies teacher have them discuss the causes of the U.S. Civil War or the consequences of the Great Depression. Students unfamiliar with both process and content are likely to shut down, and the results of attempting these conversations will be disappointing. Once students are comfortable communicating in a structured format, they will be ready to move into course content.

Teachers next need to frame the acquisition of these skills in such a way that students understand their utility in life and in the workplace. Helping students develop an ability to solve problems, make decisions, and work effectively in pairs and groups should be highly relevant to them as they ponder the future. Assisting them in an understanding of the importance of this skill set is a far more powerful framing tool than "It is important because it is on the test on Friday!" ever was. A student who graduates from high school confident in his ability to communicate and interact with peers and older adults will be able to confront life head on and succeed in a workforce that values such skills.

Ramping up relevance for today's student means attending to the realities of life and the workplace while at the same time recognizing the need for academic excellence. Beland (2007) reminds us that we as educators "need not view academic learning and social and emotional learning as opposite ends of a tug-of-war. When both support each other, students are more apt to be engaged in learning and develop themselves personally" (p. 69).

The Ultimate Motivator

Educators get so caught up in the *what* and even the *how* of teaching that we often forget about the *why*. In other words, from the perspective of students, why bother? Why should I do this? Why should I work at this? Why should I complete this project? Many students simply sleepwalk through their school years, marking time until they graduate or simply drop by the wayside when it becomes clear there is little to interest them in school. Somewhere inside kids there is something in which they are interested, an interest that motivates them to take action to accomplish something worthwhile for them. William Damon (2008) reminds us that teachers play a role in helping students "find their own 'paths to purpose'" by seeking to understand what lies beneath the surface.

Damon recommends that teachers talk with students about their hopes and aspirations, connect what is going on in school with their future plans, help students see the connections between lessons and world issues, and "introduce students to purpose in discussion of vocations" (p. 12). Common sense dictates that students are going to excel in areas where they possess a given talent. Realizing this, teachers must first recognize the talent a student possesses and then encourage her in the development of that talent. Gordon (2006) observes that we often concentrate on remedying the weaknesses of students "when the preponderance of evidence thus far is that performance improves most, and most rapidly, when the developmental focus is on strengths rather than on remediation of weaknesses" (p. 112). This is not to say that all remediation efforts should stop, but that it should be coupled with assistance and encouragement in areas where students have demonstrated talent and interest.

In many school districts, magnet schools serve as a springboard for students who may want to pursue careers related to their areas of talent and strength. That schools should help identify and encourage the talent and strengths of students is as true and relevant now as it has ever been, and we as educators must construct and maintain a road surface that provides traction for the dreams and aspirations of this and every generation of students. If relevance is in the eye of the beholder, then the beholders in our care expect no less than our full commitment to their future.

Final Thoughts

New or veteran teachers facing a new group of students in the fall would do well to invest time in thoughtful planning for what lies ahead. The days and weeks prior to the start of school, along with the first week with students, should be full of self-reflection, strategic planning, reading, and, like our fictional teacher Trey, asking questions of successful veteran teachers in order to find out what they do to sidestep obstacles in the classroom. Those obstacles are not insurmountable if teachers take the time to think ahead to what might happen and what to do if it does happen.

The most successful teachers I have seen over the years are those who have established clear procedures that become routine through constant practice, and who have invested time in building relationships within the classroom and school community. They operate on an even keel, refusing to lose their temper even under the most extreme circumstances. These teachers have learned to shift from the traditional role of information disseminator to that of process facilitator, and in so doing they have moved their students from passive observers to active participants.

These highly effective teachers understand the importance of providing gobs of meaningful feedback so that students can answer the twin questions, "Where am I now?" and "How do I get where I am going?" These teachers have learned to balance formative and summative assessments, and the students in their classes understand the nature and purpose of each. They value collaboration and constantly seek new methods of doing things in a continuous improvement journey that never ends. Above all, they take a proactive and cost-effective approach to teaching, refusing to wait on and simply react to events.

Now, let's rejoin our friend Trey, who, determined to succeed in his second year of teaching in spite of an admittedly unspectacular start, has just received some interesting news.

Epilogue

In April, in large measure because of his efforts to learn as much as possible from successful veteran teachers, books, journal articles, and his own expensive missteps, Trey made the commitment to continue teaching. Shortly before he had to sign his contract for the next school year, Mr. Crandall, the principal of a middle school in a neighboring school district, offered Trey an interview for a seventh-grade social studies position that had come open as the result of a retirement. This would involve a move from world history to United States history, a subject for which Trey had a passion.

Trey interviewed not only with Mr. Crandall, but with members of the Phoenix team with whom he would be working, assuming he was eventually offered the position. The interview lasted for the better part of an hour, and the questions asked of him by Mr. Crandall and the Phoenix team members had to do less with content and more with instructional delivery and basic educational principles. The Phoenix team was the inclusion team, and they explained that a good part of their success was related to varying their methods of instruction and assessment. For the first time, Trey found out that many kids with learning disabilities are kinesthetic learners and that movement and hands-on learning experiences had become critical components in the Phoenix team curriculum. They apparently spent their meetings talking not about discipline problems and playing the blame game, but in looking at data and discussing articles and books that suggested ways to improve instruction in every Phoenix classroom. Instruction was first and foremost, and continuous improvement was a mantra for teachers and students alike. Trey found this all refreshing and promising as far as his own future was concerned.

After doing a good deal of reflecting and then talking it over with his parents, Trey accepted the new middle school position and submitted his resignation at the old school. The drive to this new location would be a bit further than he had become used to, but his visit and interview had impressed him, as had the principal and the Phoenix team teachers. The fact that he could teach United States history was a definite plus. It was an exceptional high school U.S. history teacher who had put Trey on the path of teaching in the first place—a teacher in whose hands the past had come to life day after day in Trey's junior year.

The day after Trey signed the contract with the human resources department of his new school district, the principal called and invited him to the school for an official tour and a conversation. Arriving early the next morning, Trey once again noticed how very different this new school was from what he had gotten used to during the past year. The secretary rose to greet him, brought him a cup of coffee, and escorted him back to the principal's office. Her smile and demeanor helped Trey relax, and he realized that parents of students in this new school must enjoy entering a school office that was at once warm and welcoming.

After Trey and the principal had seated themselves and exchanged pleasantries, Mr. Crandall opened the conversation. "As we discussed a couple of weeks ago, Trey, you will be the social studies teacher on the Phoenix team, a six-person team composed of four core teachers, a special education teacher, and a teacher assistant. As you will recall, this is the inclusion team and among the hundred or so students on the team are approximately fifteen with learning disabilities. The team has been together for four years and they are outstanding in every way. Test scores are high, discipline referrals are virtually nonexistent, and the kids don't miss much school for the simple reason that they don't want to."

"That is amazing," said Trey. "I have to admit that my first year of teaching was pretty much the exact opposite of that. Our kids missed a lot of school, the test scores were low, and we consistently had someone on the suspension list. As I told you when we first met, this past year made me question whether or not I had chosen the right profession."

"I can remember my first year in teaching," said Mr. Crandall with a smile. "I went home every night wondering if teaching was for me. It wasn't until my second year in the classroom that things began to click and I have to attribute that newfound success to a wonderful mentor teacher who spent tons of quality time with me and introduced me to the concept that we teach people, not content."

"I hate to admit it, but I'm not sure I follow," said Trey, sipping some coffee.

"Many administrators will argue that getting into the curriculum guide or textbook quickly is a guarantor of success. Mrs. Slattery, my own former teacher mentor and the English teacher on your new team, by the way, convinced me to spend *at least* the first week of school learning student names quickly, establishing positive relationships, and going over classroom procedures until they became routine. I visited her classroom many times early in that year and she demonstrated exactly what facilitating process in the classroom looks like, feels like, and sounds like."

Trey put down his coffee cup and said, "Thinking back on my first year of teaching, I can see where doing those things would have helped later in the school year. I enjoyed September and simply assumed the rest of the year would be like that. It wasn't, and to be honest, I considered leaving teaching before the school year was even over."

"I felt exactly the same way, and had my second year been like the first, you and I would not be having this conversation because I would have quit," Mr. Crandall said with a smile. "Mrs. Slattery taught me that this profession is first and foremost about relationships and process. Teachers who invest in relationship-building and continuously improving process in the classroom are more often than not, in my experience, destined for success. I was impressed with you in our first meeting and I have no doubt that you will be an asset to the Phoenix team, its students, and our school."

"Thank you, Mr. Crandall," said Trey. "I look forward to meeting my new teammates at some point. Did you say that one of them is here today?"

Mr. Crandall smiled, "I did. In fact, Mrs. Slattery is in the building and would love to see you when we are done here. She is working in her classroom, and if you want to refill your coffee cup on our way out of the office, we can go see her and visit your new classroom."

Trey waited while Mr. Crandall called down to Mrs. Slattery's room to make sure she was there, and they headed in that direction. Along the way, Mr. Crandall made quick stops at the computer lab and the media center. Inside the media center was a room with a conference table and two walls filled with magazines and books, along with a long counter that housed three computers. "This is our professional development library," said Mr. Crandall. "Teachers meet here at least once per week and research instruction-related topics using the books, the journals, and the computers. Those meetings help drive instruction in the school, and this room has become a popular place as test results and student satisfaction surveys indicate that the emphasis on student engagement and learner-centered classrooms is paying off. Over the past four years we have seen scores go up considerably. Absenteeism is down among students and faculty alike, and collaboration is the norm."

"This is amazing," said Trey. "I don't remember us even having a room like this at the other middle school. If we did, I certainly did not know about it."

"We emphasize collaboration here," said Mr. Crandall, "and faculty meetings are devoted not to a series of 'talking heads' or memos, but to instruction. I can't tell you how many ideas have come from those meetings. Because we want the students up, moving, and sharing in the classrooms, I get the teachers up, moving, and sharing in those meetings. The idea is to model the kinds of interactive strategies we want to see in the classrooms. Ah, here we are . . . room 23 and Mrs. Slattery."

They entered the classroom, and what immediately hit Trey was the fact that there were no rows of student desks. Instead, there were small round tables around the perimeter of the room, with plenty of open space in the middle. Mrs. Slattery, who had moved from the back of the room to the front when they entered, seemed to read Trey's mind and said, "That space in the middle is for the students to move around in as they pair up and engage in structured conversations. That happens often and it gets noisy, but neither the students nor I would have it any other way."

Trey, who could not imagine his former students standing or sharing in this manner, could only wonder at the whole classroom setup and her explanation of its use. "I hope I can see this happen early in the year. This is all new to me," he said.

Mr. Crandall said, "You'll have opportunities to see all your teammates in action during the month of September. We'll get others to cover your classroom so that you can see several short activities and collaborative strategies in action. Mrs. Slattery, in addition to being your teammate, will be your mentor. I can tell you from experience that there is none better. You are in good hands, and speaking of that, I'll leave the two of you to chat a bit while I conduct an interview for a new nighttime custodian. Stop by the office, Trey, before you leave and I'll answer any questions you have. Welcome aboard."

"Thanks," said Trey, "and I appreciate the tour and your willingness to meet with me so soon after school is out."

"It is my pleasure. The office manager, Mrs. Ballew, will give you your room key when you want to pick it up. I'll see you soon."

Mr. Crandall left and Mrs. Slattery commented, "I always knew that man was headed for a 'big picture' job down the road. When he moved from assistant principal to principal here, he asked me to join him and put together a dynamite inclusion team for seventh grade. I must say that these past four years have been the best of a long career in teaching. Why don't we go across the hall and see your classroom, Trey? I had one of the custodians unlock the door."

They crossed to room 24 and Trey was again struck by the difference between what he was seeing and his old classroom. Once again, there were no student desks and the teacher's desk had been banished to a back corner of the room. Each of the six small round tables had four chairs with tennis balls at the bottom of the legs to allow for frequent movement without scratching the tiled floor.

After looking around a bit, Trey said, "I hope I can live up to the expectations of the Phoenix team. I must admit that all this is new to me. My first year of teaching included a lot of lecture, worksheets, and videos."

Mrs. Slattery laughed and said, "You'll be fine, Trey. When we interviewed you, we did not fail to notice your willingness to take risks on behalf of kids. Your positive attitude impressed all of us and frankly, that is what we were looking for. This is an exciting team and we have made improvements for each of the four years we have been together. I think you'll fit in just fine, Trey. We believe that awareness leads to choice. By that I mean that we are constantly seeking new instructional delivery methods based on the VAK predicates—visual, auditory, and kinesthetic. Our special education students, particularly, are highly kinesthetic and need to move, process, and get involved in hands-on activities that capitalize on their strengths as kinesthetic learners. We use tons of visuals, including graphs, charts, maps, and graphic organizers on which our visually oriented students rely. As I believe we said during your interview, we don't believe for a second that one size fits all."

Trey looked around his new classroom. "I've got the whole summer to plan for the coming year on the Phoenix team. I want to fit in and become a contributing member of what seems to be a powerful team and a great school. Do you have any suggestions?"

"Well, as we mentioned during your interview, the Phoenix team teachers meet twice in July and once early in August before everyone reports back for the new school year. The very first meeting will be during the second week of July, and it will be at my house. You'll be part of the decision as to which day we meet and I'll be in touch via e-mail. At those meetings, we take a look at the previous year and reflect on what worked and what didn't and we make some key decisions related to the coming school year."

"What can I do on my own?" asked Trey. "Frankly, I don't want to have the same problems with discipline I had in my first year. It was apparent during my interview that the Phoenix team does not generally experience those problems and I can use all the help I can get in that regard."

Mrs. Slattery paused for a moment and then said, "I'll send you an e-mail that tells you more about our team and what has made us successful over the four years we have been together, but I can tell you that the best decision we made during that first year as a team was to delay introducing content into the mix until we had established our procedures, processes, and expectations. We made a conscious effort to put process before content."

"Can you give me an example?" asked Trey.

"Yes," said Mrs. Slattery. "We have our students pair up frequently, either seated or standing, to process information related to course content. However, we spend much of the first several days in each of our classes getting students used to doing that successfully. Having structured conversations, making eye contact, and developing good listening skills requires a great deal of practice, patience, and perseverance. By the time we introduce content into those paired or group conversations, our students are quite skilled at working with each other. This pays great dividends later on for us and for them. Many twenty-first century jobs require this kind of communication and collaboration, so we are not only making our classes run more smoothly, but we are also giving them life skills that will follow them into the workforce."

"Amazing," said Trey. "The idea that we are standing here talking about these things is new to me. I look forward to meeting with everyone on the team. Any more suggestions?"

"Well," said Mrs. Slattery, "Building a solid foundation for the year includes more than just turning procedures into routines. It also means spending that first week of school building relationships with the students. In fact, we generally call the homes of our students as soon as we get the class lists in order to begin developing lasting relationships with the parents. Once again, that pays off later in the school year and, unfortunately, is something many teachers won't take the time to do."

"I get the idea that this school, under Mr. Crandall, is one where collaboration is not just a catch phrase," said Trey.

"Absolutely," said Mrs. Slattery. "Teams are required to meet on a regular basis and Mr. Crandall often attends those meetings. One of his favorite sayings is that the biggest room in the world is the room for improvement. Mr. Crandall has made a great many improvements in the building over the past four years, the most important of which are those related to instruction. He believes that in order to learn, kids must be engaged in the material and teachers must be engaged in the improvement process."

"What about tests and quizzes?" asked Trey.

"Mr. Crandall is a proponent of frequent and meaningful feedback for students. Using formative assessments and checking frequently for understanding are encouraged. He models that by meeting frequently with teachers and assisting us in our own improvement efforts. By the time we get to our own summative evaluation we have usually been able to make the adjustments necessary to improve instruction so that our evaluations are really pretty good. The same is true for the kids, by the way. If we check for understanding at many points along the way, the summative assessments will take care of themselves."

"I know you have things to do this morning," said Trey. "I'll walk you back to your room. Any final bits of advice for me?"

Mrs. Slattery thought for a moment and when they arrived at her classroom door said, "I would encourage you to reflect on your first year as a teacher. I'm not talking about content here. The content will be different for you anyway with the grade-level change, but think not so much about the *what* as you do about the *how* of teaching. Ask yourself some pointed questions related directly to how you might make changes that would result in improvement in processes and more effective instruction. In my twenty years as a teacher, I have come to the conclusion that reflection and the willingness to make necessary adjustments will benefit you and your students."

Trey looked at her and said, "Twenty years! I think that is wonderful. Honestly, I was ready to quit after my first year!"

Mrs. Slattery shook her head slowly and said, "The truth is that we are losing too many teachers because they are simply not happy in the profession. They may not have the professional development or support necessary to get past those first few years. They fight what they see as an uphill battle until they just sit down and pack it in. You said you almost went into sales, and many former teachers have done just that. I can promise you one thing in your second year. The Phoenix team will dedicate itself to your success and Mr. Crandall will support you every step of the way."

"That is great, Mrs. Slattery, and I really look forward to being on the inclusion team."

"Trey, my name is Miriam, but everyone calls me Mimi for short. Working on the inclusion team has been the best experience of my teaching career; these kids need us to build solid relationships, give them gobs of feedback, assist them with skill development, and model the kind of behavior and attitudes critical to their success. We are relentlessly positive, Trey, and we do not spend our time complaining about things beyond our control. If obstacles can be removed, we remove them or sidestep them. I think you are going to love it here and I would bet you have a long and rewarding teaching career ahead of you."

"Thanks again, Mimi, and I'll get to work right away. Mr. Crandall has a reading list for me, and that should keep me busy in the meantime. E-mail me when you are ready to schedule that first July meeting."

"I'll do that," said Mrs. Slattery, "and welcome to the Phoenix team."

Before leaving, Trey stopped at the office and arranged to take out a couple of books and journals from the professional development library. He also picked up the key to his classroom and decided to return the next day, filled with a new sense of excitement. The contrast was pronounced. His first year had ended in frustration, and that experience could well have terminated his teaching career after just nine months. Walking to his car, it occurred to him that his second year was headed in the right direction. The amount of support he anticipated at this new school contrasted sharply with his first year in the profession.

Trey's brush with burnout had been replaced with the near certainty that his year would be different and his teaching career might be a long one after all. Trey and his Phoenix teammates met in July at Mimi Slattery's house to do some preliminary planning for the coming school year. In all, they met three times at various locations before the teachers reported back near the end of August. By the end of October, he realized that this new experience would define his remaining days as a teacher, no matter where his career might lead him down the road. Mrs. Slattery was a wonderful mentor who took time to reflect with Trey on everything from instructional delivery to organization. From day one, Mr. Crandall made it clear that there was no room in the climate of the school for a negative attitude or the blame game. This positive, proactive, can-do climate permeated the building and affected teachers and students alike.

Appendix

Preparing for Day Six

Trey was fortunate enough to change schools at a time when his energy level and sense of accomplishment were at low ebb. His new principal and teacher mentor provided the support he needed to succeed. Not only did Trey ultimately succeed, he was in a position to become a strong teacher leader several years into his career. Too many teachers reach the end of that first year and simply sit down and quit trying. Many, perhaps a large percentage, of those young teachers could succeed if they understood the critical role that preparation, reflection, and informed decisions play in that ultimate success.

While teachers may have little say in the *what* of teaching, the *how* is usually left up to them. School boards, administrators, and state assessments may dictate the core curriculum in terms of content, but teachers normally have the latitude to decide how that content will be delivered. The key is to understand just how important climate and delivery are to learning. Perhaps too many administrators and teachers, according to Blankstein (2004), ask, "Who has time for these things when the 'real' work of increasing student achievement awaits?"

Who has the time to take a full five days at the beginning of school in order to establish and practice procedures? Who has the time to delay introducing course content until behavioral expectations are discussed, clearly understood, and agreed upon by teachers and students alike? Who has time to make a solid start at creating a safe classroom climate that is conducive to learning? Who has the time to explain to students the difference between summative and formative assessments in a way that allows students to understand the nature and uses of feedback? Who has time to discuss with students the relevance of what they will be doing for the next nine months? The answer to all these questions is *any teacher who wants to succeed with his or her students and stay in the profession for the long haul.* Teachers who are unwilling to take a *proactive* approach to planning both *before* and *during* that first week of school are likely to spend the rest of the school year waiting on events and *reacting* to crises as fall fades into winter and the problems multiply.

Trey's Phoenix team partners served as a great support mechanism for him in his second year of teaching, in stark contrast to his lonely and frustrating first year in the profession. His new principal encouraged and supported a collegial atmosphere at his school, and Trey became part of a team that was willing to take risks and support each other in turn. Continuous improvement was more than just a phrase with them, and Trey and his students flourished because of that positive outlook and considerable synergy.

While Trey was painfully aware that he had not enjoyed that degree of support during his first year of teaching at the other school, there are some things he might have done to improve things in his own classroom even if his old teammates were not receptive to being part of Trey's efforts at improvement. It is possible that if Trey had taken the lead in that first year, others on his team might have followed, albeit slowly and hesitatingly. It is even possible that his success over the course of that and subsequent years could have reenergized and, to a considerable extent, rebuilt what had been a dysfunctional team. Trey spent his first year in reactive mode, an uncomfortable situation where forward progress in terms of student achievement is unlikely at best.

Chances are that any member of any faculty can find at least one learning partner at school—another positive, risk-taking teacher with vision and a desire to accomplish much. This ad hoc team could include more than two teachers, of course, and there is no doubt that the synergy that comes from multiple perspectives can be a powerful change agent.

This brings us to you and your own situation as a new or veteran teacher. If a wonderful support system already exists in your school, so much the better. If not, my suggestion is that you create your own vehicle for change and get as many teachers on board as possible for your continuous improvement journey. That done, what follows is a list of annotated suggestions that are calculated to assist you all the way from now to that sixth day of school (when subject area content is folded into an already functioning system replete with rules and procedures). If you are reading this book well into the school year, don't wait until next year before implementing change. Effective processes can be put in place at any time if you are willing to take a few days to make the changes.

Once you have chosen a learning partner (or multiple learning partners) from among members of your faculty, agree to do the following:

Keep an electronic journal during the course of the school year. Take a few minutes each evening to record in a file anything related to the *how* of each day's lessons. Make a list of occasions on which time seemed to be wasted getting students engaged in a given task. Were procedures always clear to students? Were there times when a set of visual instructions might have provided support to auditory directions for an activity? Were there plenty of opportunities for auditory or visual feedback for students? Did students have plenty of time to process information in class, either in pairs or teams?

Spend thirty minutes per week reading professional journals and books. Teachers may not have time to do original research, but the good news is that there are those who have written articles and books that incorporate the latest research in the field of education. We want our doctors to be perfectly familiar with the latest research in the field of medicine and we want our auto mechanics to know what makes our engines tick. It is reasonable for parents and students to expect that we will be conversant with current research in the area of teaching and learning.

Find time to watch each other teach. It is often impossible for teachers to get a balcony view of their own classrooms. Work it out so that you have multiple opportunities to observe your new teammates and to have them sit in on your classes. Rather than watching your teacher-friend work, spend most of the time watching the students. Answer some basic process-related questions about your observation: Did students appear to be engaged? Did students process information by talking with each other? If not, did you notice opportunities for student-to-student conversations? Did the teacher use music to facilitate process? If not, were there times when music might have been used? Were posted rules followed?

Schedule time to meet with other teachers frequently. Meet on a regularly scheduled basis with your teammates and use that time to incorporate the observations from your journal entries, the latest research on multiple topics, and your classroom observation notes into your conversation. Specifically, zero in on those things that directly affect learning: classroom climate, rules and procedures, feedback, formative assessment, diverse delivery methods, learning styles, and the importance of relevance, to name a few. Focus on one topic per meeting and see if you can come to a consensus on what each of you could change in your classrooms that would have a positive affect on learning. Institute the changes and then spend some time at the next meeting discussing the results. Don't forget to celebrate the results.

Take time in class to have your students give you feedback. For the most part, you will see a new group of students each school year. While they are new to you, they are veteran students. That is, they know full well which of their former teachers where excellent, good, average, or below average. Spend some time each week or at least once monthly finding out how things are going for them in your classroom. Is there too much "teacher talk" and too little student involvement in the day-to-day classroom routine? Do students feel you are using enough graphic organizers or other visuals to provide clarity and facilitate understanding? Do they think you are providing enough movement in class? Is it their opinion that you provide enough feedback on homework assignments, quizzes, and tests? Teachers often hesitate to ask these questions for the simple reason that they are afraid of the answers. The truth is that no one can improve without considerable introspection and tons of feedback. Feedback is the lubricant of a smooth-running educational engine.

Final Thoughts

In the summer of 2007, I stained our fence. It was quite a job because my fence is composed of fifty-two eight-foot panels, meaning there were one hundred and four segments that needed stained! The fence, built of salt-treated lumber, had not been stained in many years, and it looked every bit like it. I decided to use a chocolate brown, semi-transparent stain to accomplish the task, and from the beginning it was clear to me that this job was going to take many weeks. Each eight-foot section took an hour to complete with two coats of stain.

That first morning, it took me until almost noon to complete three sections of fence, and when I stood back and looked at those three panels, I was greatly satisfied with both my effort and the result. It looked, to me, magnificent; on most mornings from then on I arose at dawn and went outside, until after three weeks the entire interior of the fence was finished. Again, I was struck by how beautiful it looked, and during many a summer evening I stood on my back porch and looked with a mounting sense of accomplishment at what I had done.

I suppose my mission statement for staining the fence went something like this: "My mission, using the best available technology, is to properly prepare my fence for the twenty-first century." But it wasn't the mission statement that got me up at the crack of dawn each summer morning. Every evening I stood in my yard and marveled at what I had accomplished, gazing with pride at the steady march of progress. The visual image of that progress gave me great satisfaction, and it provided vision. Knowing that each day would bring considerable improvement actually motivated me to get up early each summer morning.

As teachers, we live for the moment that the kids get it. We revel in their understanding, and we gain strength and encouragement from our own role in their steady progress. We did not enter teaching for the money; any teacher who did that did not read the fine print. When, as a seventh-grade teacher on the inclusion team, I saw one of my students do something today he could not do yesterday, I was reminded of why I loved working with the kids and adults that comprised our middle school family.

Yes, there were days when I shook my head in disbelief over this or that, and there were afternoons when a nap seemed in order on returning home. There were days when I wondered if I was connecting at all, and there were evenings when grading essays and tests required an infusion of caffeine. In the final analysis, however, looking into the faces of kids who understood, or sought to understand, provided all the incentive I needed to rise with the sun, crank up my favorite songs on a cassette player or CD, and get to school in order to help more of my students, in hopes that they would accomplish something they had not been able to do yesterday.

My final piece of advice to teachers—new and veteran alike—is to provide moments of personal reflection that allow you to see in your mind's eye just what you are accomplishing from day to day. Seeing the lightbulb go off in the eyes of even a few kids at a time will provide a powerful and lasting image that, in its turn, illuminates the vision you have created for you and the students in your care.

References

Allen, R. (2002). *Impact teaching: Ideas and strategies for teachers to maximize student learning.* Boston: Allyn & Bacon.

Armstrong, T. (2006). *The best schools: How human development research should inform educational practice.* Alexandria, VA: Association for Supervision and Curriculum Development.

Bailey, B. (2000). *Conscious discipline: 7 basic skills for brain smart classroom management.* Oviedo, FL: Loving Guidance.

Barth, R. (2001). *Learning by heart.* San Francisco: Jossey-Bass.

Beland, K. (2007). Boosting social and emotional competence. *Educational Leadership, 64*(7), 68–71.

Black, P., & William, D. (1998). Inside the black box: Raising standards through classroom assessment. *Phi Delta Kappan, 80*(2), 139–148.

Blankstein, A. (2004). *Failure is NOT an option: Six principles that guide student achievement in high-performing schools.* Thousand Oaks, CA: Corwin.

Blaydes Madigan, J. (2004). *Thinking on your feet* (2nd ed.). Murphy, TX: Action Based Learning.

Bluestein, J. (1999). *21st century discipline: Teaching students responsibility and self-management.* Torrance, CA: Fearon Teacher Aids.

Bluestein, J. (2001). *Creating emotionally safe schools: A guide for educators and parents.* Deerfield Beach, FL: Health Communications.

Bosworth, K. (1995). Caring for others and being cared for: Students talk caring in school. *Phi Delta Kappan, 76,* 686–693.

Boynton, M., & Boynton, C. (2005). *The educator's guide to preventing and solving discipline problems.* Alexandria, VA: Association for Supervision and Curriculum Development.

Bozzone, M. (1996). My colleagues NEVER drive me crazy: How teachers at one school said goodbye to gripes, boosted morale, and built a bastion of faculty unity. *Instructor, 105*(5), 54–59.

Brookhart, S. (2007/2008). Feedback that fits. *Educational Leadership, 65*(4), 54–59.

Brookhart, S. (2008). *How to give effective feedback to your students.* Alexandria, VA: Association for Supervision and Curriculum Development.

Brooks, J., & Brooks, M. (1999). *In search of understanding: The case for constructivist classrooms.* Alexandria, VA: Association for Supervision and Curriculum Development.

Brophy, J. (1981). Teacher praise: A functional analysis. *Review of Educational Research, 51*, 5–32.

Brophy, J., & Evertson, C. M. (1976). *Learning from teaching: A developmental perspective.* Boston: Allyn & Bacon.

Brown, D. (2005). The significance of congruent communication in effective classroom management. *The Clearing House, 79*(1), 12–15.

Brown, J. S. (2000). Growing up digital: How the web changes work, education, and the ways people learn. *Change, 32*(2), 11–20.

Burke, K. (2005). *How to assess authentic learning.* (4th ed.). Thousand Oaks, CA: Corwin.

Burke, K. (2006). *From standards to rubrics in 6 steps: Tools for assessing student learning, K–8.* Thousand Oaks, CA: Corwin.

Carr, J. F., & Harris, D. E. (2001). *Succeeding with standards: Linking curriculum, assessment, and action planning.* Alexandria, VA: Association for Supervision and Curriculum Development.

Charles, C. M. (2002). *Essential elements of effective discipline.* Boston, MA: Allyn & Bacon.

Charles, C. M., & Charles, M. G. (2004). *Classroom management for middle-grades teachers.* Boston: Pearson Education.

Costa, A. (2008). *The school as a home for the mind: Creating mindful curriculum, instruction, and dialogue.* Thousand Oaks, CA: Corwin.

Crew, J. (1969, Spring). The effect of study strategies on the retention of college text material. *Journal of Reading Behavior, 1*(2), 45–52.

Curwin, R. L. (2003). *Making good choices: Developing responsibility, respect, and self-discipline in Grades 4–9.* Thousand Oaks, CA: Corwin.

Damon, W. (2008, October). The moral north star: How do we help students understand that academic excellence can get them where they want to go? *Educational Leadership, 66*(2), 8–12.

Deci, E. (1996). *Why we do what we do: Understanding self-motivation.* London: Penguin Books.

Depka, E. (2006). *The data guidebook for teachers and leaders: Tools for continuous improvement.* Thousand Oaks, CA: Corwin.

Dicks, M. J. (2005, November). Show me the way. *Educational Leadership, 63*(3), 78–80.

Di Giulio, R. C. (2007). *Positive classroom management: A step-by-step guide to helping students succeed* (3rd ed.). Thousand Oaks, CA: Corwin.

Donaldson, G. A., Jr. (2001). *Cultivating leadership in schools: Connecting people, purpose, and practice.* New York: Teachers College.

Eaker, R., DuFour, R., & DuFour, R. (2002). *Getting started: Reculturing schools to become professional learning communities.* Bloomington, IN: National Education Service.

Ehrlich, R., & Zoltek, S. (2006). It's not wrong to tell students when they're wrong. *Journal of College Science Teaching, 35*(4), 8–10.

Emmer, E. T., Evertson, C. M., & Worsham, M. E. (2003). *Classroom management for secondary teachers* (6th ed.). Boston: Allyn & Bacon.

Evans, R. (2004). *Family matters: How schools can cope with the crisis in childrearing.* San Francisco: Jossey-Bass.

Feinstein, S. (2004). *Secrets of the teenage brain.* Thousand Oaks, CA: Corwin.

Fisher, D., & Frey, N. (2007). *Checking for understanding: Formative assessment techniques for your classroom.* Alexandria, VA: Association for Supervision and Curriculum Development.

Fogarty, R. (1990). *Designs for cooperative interactions.* Thousand Oaks, CA: Corwin.

Fullan, M. (2005). *Leadership & sustainability: System thinkers in action.* Thousand Oaks, CA: Corwin.

Garmston, R., & Wellman, B. (1999). *The adaptive school: A sourcebook for developing collaborative groups.* Norwood, MA: Christopher-Gordon.

Garner, B. K. (2007). *Getting to "Got it!" Helping struggling students learn how to learn.* Alexandria, VA: Association for Supervision and Curriculum Development.

Gewertz, C. (2008, October). States press ahead on '21st-century skills'. *Education Week, 28*(8), 21, 23.

Goleman, D. (1995). *Emotional intelligence.* New York: Bantam Books.

Goleman, D. (2006). *Social intelligence: The revolutionary new science of human relationships.* New York: Bantam Dell.

Good, T., & Brophy, J. (1984). *Looking in classrooms* (3rd ed.). New York: Harper & Row.

Goodlad, J. I. (2004). *A place called school* (2nd ed.). New York: McGraw-Hill.

Gordon, G. (2006). *Building engaged schools: Getting the most out of America's classrooms.* New York: Gallup Press.

Gregory, G. (2005). *Differentiating instruction with style: Aligning teacher and learner intelligences for maximum achievement.* Thousand Oaks, CA: Corwin.

Grinder, M. (2006). *A healthy classroom* (2nd ed.). Battle Ground, WA: Michael Grinder & Associates.

Hannaford, C. (2005). *Smart moves: Why learning is not all in your head.* Salt Lake City, UT: Great River Books.

Harrison, C., & Killion, J. (2007, September). Ten roles for teacher leaders. *Educational Leadership, 65*(1), 74.

Hattie, J., & Temperley, H. (2007). The power of feedback. *Review of Educational Research, 77,* 81–112.

Hord, S. M., & Sommers, W. A. (2008). *Leading professional learning communities: Voices from research and practice.* Thousand Oaks, CA: Corwin.

Jenkins, L. (2003). *Improving student learning: Applying Deming's quality principles in classrooms* (2nd ed.). Milwaukee, WI: ASQ Quality Press.

Jenkins, L. (2005). *Permission to forget and nine other root causes of America's frustration with education.* Milwaukee, WI: ASQ Quality Press.

Jensen, E. (2005). *Teaching with the brain in mind* (2nd ed.). Alexandria, VA: Association for Supervision and Curriculum Development.

Johnston, P. H. (2004). *Choice words: How our language affects children's learning.* Portland, ME: Stenhouse.

Jones, F. (2007). *Tools for teaching.* Santa Cruz, CA: Fredric H. Jones & Associates.

Kaufeldt, M. (2005). *Teachers, change your bait! Brain-compatible differentiated instruction.* Bethel, CT: Crown House.

Kohn, A. (1999). *The schools our children deserve: Moving beyond traditional classrooms and "tougher standards."* New York: Houghton Mifflin.

Konold, K. E., Miller, S. P., & Konold, K. B. (2004). Using teacher feedback to enhance student learning. *Teaching Exceptional Children, 36*(6), 64–69.

Koutoufas, L. (2007). Lessons from the second year: What I learned from second grade. In P. Bigler & S. Bishop (Eds.), *Be a teacher: You can make a difference.* (pp. 106–121). St. Petersburg, FL: Vandamere Press.

Liesveld, R., & Miller, J. A. (2005). *Teach with your strengths: How great teachers inspire their students.* New York: Gallup Press.

Lipton, L., & Wellman, B. (2000). *Pathways to understanding: Patterns and practices in the learning-focused classroom.* Guilford, VT: Pathways.

Lipton, L., & Wellman, B. (2001). *Mentoring matters: A practical guide to learning-focused relationships.* Sherman, CT: Mira Via.

Little, J. W. (1990, Summer). The persistence of privacy: Autonomy and initiative in teachers' professional relations. *Teachers College Record, 91*(4), 509–536.

Maeroff, G. I. (1993). *Team building for school change: Equipping teachers for new roles.* New York: Teachers College Press.

Marzano, R. (2003a). *Classroom management that works: Research-based strategies for every teacher.* Alexandria, VA: Association for Supervision and Curriculum Development.

Marzano, R. (2003b). *What works in schools: Translating research into action.* Alexandria, VA: Association for Supervision and Curriculum Development.

Marzano, R. (2006). *Classroom assessment and grading that work.* Alexandria, VA: Association for Supervision and Curriculum Development.

Marzano, R. (2007). *The art and science of teaching: A comprehensive framework for effective instruction.* Alexandria, VA: Association for Supervision and Curriculum Development.

Marzano, R., Pickering, D., & Pollock, J. (2001). *Classroom instruction that works: Research-based strategies for increasing student achievement.* Alexandria, VA: Association for Supervision and Curriculum Development.

McCombs, B. L., & Whisler, J. S. (1997). *The learner-centered classroom and school: Strategies for increasing student motivation and achievement.* San Francisco: Jossey-Bass.

Mitra, D. L. (2008, November). Amplifying student voice: Students have much to tell us about how best to reform our schools. *Educational Leadership, 66*(3), 20–25.

Nash, R. (2008). *The active classroom: Practical strategies for involving students in the learning process.* Thousand Oaks, CA: Corwin.

O'Neill, J., & Conzemius, A. (2006). *The power of smart goals: Using goals to improve student learning.* Bloomington, IN: Solution Tree.

Popham, W. J. (2008). *Transformative assessment.* Alexandria, VA: Association for Supervision and Curriculum Development.

Rader, L. (2005, January/February). Goal setting for students and teachers: Six steps to success. *The Clearing House, 78*(3), 123–126.

Ratey, J. (2008). *Spark: The revolutionary new science of exercise and the brain.* New York: Little, Brown and Company.

Reason, C., & Reason, L. (2007, September). Asking the right questions. *Educational Leadership, 65*(1), 36.

Regan, B. (2008, July). Why we need to teach 21st century skills--And how to do it. *MultiMedia & Internet@Schools, 15*(4), 10–13. Retrieved December 9, 2008, from Education Periodicals database at www.proquest.umi.com (Document ID: 1509933481).

Rooney, J. (2006, September). Unleashing the energy. *Educational Leadership, 64*(1), 91–92.

Schmoker, M. (1999). *Results: The key to continuous school improvement* (2nd ed.). Alexandria, VA: Association for Supervision and Curriculum Development.

Sergiovanni, T. J. (2005). *Strengthening the heartbeat: Leading and learning together in schools.* San Francisco: Jossey-Bass.

Smith, R. (2004). *Conscious classroom management: Unlocking the secrets of great teaching.* Fairfax, CA: Conscious Teaching.

Sousa, D. A. (2001). *How the brain learns* (2nd ed.). Thousand Oaks, CA: Corwin.

Sprenger, M. (2005). *How to teach so students remember.* Alexandria, VA: Association for Supervision and Curriculum Development.

Tate, M. (2007). *Shouting won't grow dendrites.* Thousand Oaks, CA: Corwin.

Thorson, S. A. (2003). *Listening to students: Reflections on secondary classroom management.* Boston: Allyn & Bacon.

Tileson, D. W. (2004). *What every teacher should know about student motivation.* Thousand Oaks, CA: Corwin.

Tomlinson, C., & Jarvis, J. (2006, September). Teaching beyond the book. *Educational Leadership. 64*(1), 16–21.

Tomlinson, C., & McTighe, J. (2006). *Integrating differentiated instruction & understanding by design: Connecting content and kids.* Alexandria, VA: Association for Supervision and Curriculum Development.

Vosniadou, S., Ioannides, C., Dimitrakopoulou, A., & Papademetriou, E. (2001). Designing learning environments to promote conceptual change in science. *Learning and Instruction, 11*, 381–419.

Wagner, T. (2008a). *The global achievement gap.* New York: Basic Books.

Wagner, T. (2008b). Rigor redefined. *Educational Leadership, 66*(2), 20–24.

Werts, M. G., Wolery, M., Gast, D. L., & Holcombe, A. (1996). Sneak in some extra learning by using instructive feedback. *Teaching Exceptional Children, 28*(3), 70–71.

Witmer, M. (2005). The fourth R in education—relationships. *The Clearing House, 78*(5), 224–228.

Wolfe, P. (2001). *Brain matters: Translating research into classroom practice.* Alexandria, VA: Association for Supervision and Curriculum Development.

Wong, H., & Wong, R. (2005). *How to be an effective teacher: The first days of school.* Mountain View, CA: Harry K. Wong.

Woods, A. M., & Weasmer, J. (2002, March/April). Maintaining job satisfaction: Engaging professionals as active participant. *Clearing House, 75*(4), 186–189.

Zmuda, A., Kuklis, R., & Kline, E. (2004). *Transforming schools: Creating a culture of continuous improvement.* Alexandria, VA: Association for Supervision and Curriculum Development.

Index

CORWIN
A SAGE Company

The Corwin logo—a raven striding across an open book—represents the union of courage and learning. Corwin is committed to improving education for all learners by publishing books and other professional development resources for those serving the field of PreK–12 education. By providing practical, hands-on materials, Corwin continues to carry out the promise of its motto: **"Helping Educators Do Their Work Better."**